The Autobiography of Junior Hodge

The Autobiography of Junior Hodge

His Life in Washington D.C.

Charles R. Hodge, Jr.

2005

The Autobiography of Junior Hodge

To Mary
God Bless you in all
that you do. Enjoy
Reading this work
Nice joining with you

Charles R. Hodge Jr.

28 Feb 2017

THE TRAIN

My first recollection of my childhood life was in the year of our Lord and Savior Jesus Christ 1943. I was approximately three or four year's old, my family was living in a house with my aunt Virginia and Uncle Russell on Virginia Avenue and Third Street in South East Washington D.C. I can remember clearly when my sister and I used to play on a dirt parking lot near the tent grounds on Virginia Avenue. The railroad underground exit was across the street from the fair grounds leading into the coal yard. When my sister and I heard the loud sound of the whistle blowing from the locomotive, we would run across the street to the bridge and hang over the four foot concrete stone wall to see and count each train as it came out of the tunnel. The most exciting part of this train experience was to count each train as it exited the tunnel, and to be the first person to identify the red and black caboose (the last train traveling behind the locomotive on the railroad track). We would sometimes stand on the dangerous concrete wall and hold onto the chain link fence while counting each train as it came out of the tunnel loaded with tons of coal for the coal yard

OUR MOVE TO THE PROJECT HOUSING;

Our family moved from my aunt and uncle's house on Virginia Avenue S.E. to the new Frederick Douglass Housing Dwellings. The address to our new house was 1802 Stanton Terrace, South East Washington D.C. Our new house was a brick two-bedroom, one-bath small attached townhouse in the projects. The kitchen in our house was built below-ground with a living room and a wooden/coal stove for heating. Our house was located in a half-moon circle with four housing units, each subdivision contain a three family dwelling. We lived in one of the center units. At the rear of our house there was a chain link fence separating our house from three small 2 to 3 acre farms and each of them had a variety of the following; fruit trees, apples, peaches, cherries and pears. They also had a variety of farm animals, chickens, cows, horses, turkeys, goats, rabbits, pigs, cats and a few dogs.

THE OLD LADY'S PEARS;

I remember this old lady who had a farm house with a little garden and a few pear trees in the back of our house, whom we called Old Lady Rotten Apple because she appeared to display a mien attitude, Almost all of the children in the neighborhood thought that she was a wicked old witch from the east who did not like children. We all thought that she would beat you up or shoot us if she caught you trying to steal fruit from one of her fruit trees in her back yard. I remember on one occasion a group of children in our neighborhood decided to go over the fence a pick some pears off of her pear tree. Four or five of us climbed over the fence and began picking pears she spotted us and came running out the back door of her house with a loaded double-barreled shot gun in her hand. I heard a loud bang or pop like noise that came from her double-barreled shotgun. We started to run as fast as we could because we did not know if she was shooting at us or shooting in the air, but we were not sticking around to find out. We scattered like scared chickens, we ran towards the 6 foot high chain link fence. We leaped over that six-foot chain linked fence with one hop, skip and a jump. We would grab the top of the fence with both hands and push our feet into the chain link that would give us the spring to take us over the fence. We were so scared of the experience we encounter with that old lady, we made a covenant never to tell our parents of this adventure for fear of being switched and punished. Over the years, I became a friend of the old lady and found out that she had a heart of pure gold and truly loved children. When asked why did she come out shooting when the children were in her garden she stated that she did not want to hurt anyone all she wanted to do was scare the children to stop them from stealing her fruit. She told me that if they would have only asked her for some pears, she would have gladly allowed them to pick what they could eat. The lessons I learned from this experience was not to pre judge people, give everybody a chance, if you want something bad enough simply ask for it, grow your own or simply employ yourself to buy the things you want. There is a penalty you must pay if you try and steal something that does not belong to you.

MR. MAC'S FRUIT TREES

I remember Mr. Mac, who owned a farm that was located directly behind our house. I always loved and anticipated fall season in Washington D.C. The weather always seem to be perfect: not too hot and not too cold. In the fall of the year the weather was just right. The leaves were changing colors and the air had a fragrance smell of sweet of roses mixed with scent of ripe pears and apples. That extraordinary smell in the air gave me the feeling of wanting to be suspended in that time zone for ever. The early mornings were crisp and cool, with the smell of fresh cool air and a mist of dew covering the green grass, pretty flowers and our vegetable gardens. In the early morning it seems as though everything was still asleep and waiting for the Almighty God to raise his sun into the sky to start a new day. I waited with anticipation for the dawn of a new day. In a moment of time every living creature created by God would come alive as soon as the sun rays began to peak over the horizon. The dew would be sucked up into the clouds. The sound of cock crowing would be the first sound of the day that alerts all God's creation that this is a dawning of the new day. The ants and other insect would move and go to work in their environment. Mom would start her day by lifting up all the window shades in the kitchen and throughout the rest of the house to let God's sunlight shine in. Dad's started his day in the bathroom shaving his face and grooming him self before leaving home to go to work. My father seems to be running late everyday. He was always in a rush to eat his breakfast fast so that he would be on time to catch the six o-clock bus to work. As soon the front door slammed behind dad, mom would wake us up to start our daily chores the day and to prepare ourselves for school. I was always the first one to wake up in the morning at the sound of the roosters welcoming in a new day. My mind was always thinking about how I was going to get across the change link that separated our back yard from Mr. Mac's farm to get some of the ripe pears on the ground that had fallen over night off Mr. Mac's pear tree. As soon as the first light of day appeared, the rooster would crow "Cock-a doo-doo-do!" That was my queue wake up and put on my old cut-off short pants, cotton t-shirt and a pair of old rotten smelly and holey tennis shoes. I departed out of the back door of my house and walked down the, slippery muddy clay path through the bushes and weeds to the silver gray chain link fence separating Mr. Mac Property from ours. I scouted the entire area to make sure that the coast was clear, and to ensure that Buster (Mr. Mac's dog) was chained to the big oak tree. Buster was a dangerous mean old black dog who would attack anything or anybody that came within the length of his steel dog chain. Early in the morning just before the break of dawn I climbed over the chain link fence and began gathering the pears and apples that had fallen onto the ground the night before. I fill up my pant pockets to the brim. I even filled my t-shirt with as much fruit as it could hold Those apples and pears were the most tastiest fruit I can remember eating, Since that time, I have never found a pear or apple that tasted as good as those I took from the trees from Mr. Mac's farm.

THE BRANCH;

There were no recreational swimming pools in the suburbs of South East Washington D.C. There were many public swimming pools throughout the D. C. area, but 99% of them were for whites only. As a child, I did not understand why the people who ran the public swimming pools and playgrounds would have some outrages excuse for not allowing us utilize the public pool facilities. Their favorite excuse or lie was to tell us that the pool had reached it maximum capacity. We tried to eliminate that by arriving at the pool 2 hours before it open. Being the first in line we thought we had it made until the recreation department manager formed another line and allowed the white to come in and ignored us blacks after standing in line for two or three hours. To this day it puzzle me why the white recreation staff was ashamed to tell us blacks that the public swimming pool paid with our parents taxes was for whites only. The only two places I can remember where blacks could go swimming were at Bannker and Spingon High School in North East and North West Washington D.C. or at the Carl's or Sparrows Beach, Fort Smallwood, Sandy Point or Atlantic City for a dip in the cold Atlantic Ocean.

Our favorite swimming hole was located in a wooded area we call the branch off of Mississippi Avenue between the military firing range and the basic training area by Camp Simms. During that time, our country was in between World War II and the Korean War. Camp Simms was an active basic training base used by the Army to provide basic military training to new military inductees. We had to go through the woods and cross a large mud flat area on our way to our special swimming hole. On our way to the swimming hole we would always stop at the mud flats to bathe in the warm brown mud. We would take off all of our clothes and submerge ourselves up to our necks in the warm mud... The temperature of the mud was between 90 and 100 degrees. To be enclosed in the hot mud was an experience I will never forget. I used to think that God had his protecting arms around me. I have never since felt as secure as I did when I was enclosed with God in the hot mud. We used to wade and play in the mud for hours before going to our swimming hole. I believe the mud in that flat had some cleaning and healing properties in it. When we left the mud flats, our bodies felt as though we just received a complete body massage. All of the young boys in the neighborhood would go swimming in the branch. The branch was a stream approximately one mile from the main road. The stream was on the Maryland side of Mississippi Avenue. Our swimming hole was in an area between two trees that appeared to have been cut down by beavers. I couldn't swim, and used to play at the water's edge. There was a deep area in the middle of the swimming hole. An old broken tree extended out about three feet out over the middle of our swimming hole, and most of the boys who could swim would use the broken tree as a diving board. One day we were having a good time until six bullies from Stanton Terrace took over the water hole, and was making all the little boys dive off the log. They told us to show them how well we could dive. When they demanded that I dive off the log, I refused. I began to cry, because I knew I could not swim if the bullies made me jump off the log into the deep part there was no doubt in my mind I would drown. I was so scared with fear of being thrown into the deep part of the swimming hole; I didn't know what to do. My mind was moving at 90 miles a minute. All I could think about was what my mother had told me: "Do not go swimming in the branch, because you could drown in the deep water". The bully and his boys picked me up and threw me into the deepest part of the swimming hole. I was struggling to keep my head above water. I panicked, as I was struggling for my life. The bullies were laughing and making fun of me struggling to try and stay on top of the water and trying get out of the swimming hole. The more I struggled to stay on top, the deeper I went under, and as I was about to give up, one of my friends pulled me out of the water. I took off, running through the woods like a naked jack rabbit. I escaped, and was headed towards the edge of the woods near the road leading to my house. When I got to the edge of the woods, I couldn't go anywhere because I was naked. I couldn't walk through the neighborhood without any clothing on. I would get a whipping from my parents, because they had fore warned me that I would get a beating if I went swimming in the branch. I was afraid to go home, so I head in the bushes, scared and trying to think what to do next. While I was hiding in the bushes, I saw the bullies coming up the pathway. I got an adrenaline rush; it seemed as though I became strong and brave, and I was no longer afraid. I grabbed a big stick and a brick, and ran out of the bushes towards the bullies. I told them that if they did not give me my clothes, I would beat them with my stick and tell my mother and father what they had done to me. Back in those days, if someone told their parents that someone tried to hurt them, the entire neighborhood would be up in arms to get the culprit, who would get a good whipping from their parents as punishment. The whole neighborhood would know about it. The bullies took off. After about an hour or so, I heard someone talking and laughing coming down the path in the woods. It was my three friends with my clothes. They told me that the bullies had taken another path, and had been gone for some time. I put on my clothes, went home, and never discussed what happened to me at the branch.

THE CAMP SIMMS FIRING RANGE

I remember when our gang would go down to the Camp Simms's firing range to look at all the pornographic pictures of naked women drawn on the walls by military personnel station at Camp Simms. The pictures were of women in suggestive poses, with their legs spread out and bending over the open water pipes that were protruding out of the cement retaining walls. Our purpose for going the firing range was to dig for lead to sell it to the junk yard. The lead from the bullets was lodge in the dirt hills directly behind the paper target area. After leaving the target area, we would go to the dump and play with the dangerous chemicals and anything else we could find. We would to take large pieces of rock lye and toss them into the water to see it the chemical reaction when the lye touches the water. The water would begin to foam, bubble and make cracking sounds. We didn't know what we were doing or how dangerous it was handling raw chemicals without body protection. We would gather several small pieces of raw lye and transport it in our pockets, not knowing that the moisture from our bodies would start a chemical reaction. By the time we got home, the lye had eaten small holes in our pants pockets, and I had several small chemical burns from the lye on my thigh. I didn't know that the lye I were carrying in my pants pockets was the cause of the burns on my legs and holes in our clothes, We finally realizes that the rock lye was dangerous when one of my friends put a couple pieces of rocks lye into a glass of water to pretend he was Dracula. He took to drink the liquid lye, and immediately the lye began to melt his lips on contact. The Public Health Department was called in to investigate this incident, and wanted to know where we got the toxic lye. We took them to the military dump where the lye was stored. As far as I know, after the investigation the Health department did not do anything and the toxic substance remained there for several years or until the construction of the Parkland Apartments. The mouth of the young boy who drank the liquid lye was disfigured for life. My friends and I continue to visit the military dump site and playing with the dangerous substance and looking for anything to sell to the junk man. For years after, the military dump was accessible to the public.

THE DISTRICT OF COLUMBIA PUBLIC SCHOOL

The public school system in the Washington D.C. is a three-tier school system: Elementary, Junior High and High school. The first day I remember attending school was in the fall season September 1945. The first day of the school year in Washington D.C. began on the first day after the Labor Day Holiday. Garfield Elementary School was the first school I attended was located at 1600 Alabama Ave S. E. Washington D.C. On our first day at school, we were instructed to form a line according to the class assignment list that was posted on the wall near the front door of the school. The boys and girls had separate entrances. I have always wondered why the boys' had to form a line in the front of the girl's entrance of the school. Embedded in concrete above the entrance door was the words girl's entrance. The girl's entrance had words embedded in concrete boy's entrance above the entrance door at the rear of the school. On my first day in my kindergarten class, my teacher Ms Jones assigned each child to his or her special little brown table. Each table was round and made of brown oak wood, approximately 21 inches high, with four to six little square four-leg get wooden chairs standing about 18 inches high round table. The chairs were too high, for your legs to fit under the table. You had to either sit sideways or lean up to the table to be comfortable. Our teacher didn't have a teaching plan for us. We were not taught phonics, basic numbers, or the alphabets. The only thing I can remember being taught in the kindergarten was how to draw and color in blank pictures. Kindergartens in that day seem to be geared for baby sitting instead of a learning environment. Each school day at noon, our teacher would declare a lunch period, she would call students by their numbered table to come to the front of the class room to get our bag lunch out of a large metal container called the lunch box. I was assigned to table number two, and was the second group of children to be called to go to the lunch box to retrieve our lunch bags from the lunch box. My sandwiches were always made with homemade biscuits covered with margarine, Kings Syrup and two pieces of strick of lean wrap in a Wonder Bread bag. Strick of lean was a piece of pork fat taken from the bottom of a pig's stomach. The meat was sliced thin and looked like a piece of bacon because it had a little piece of lean meat in the center of the fat.. When I arrived to the lunch box on the table I would reach my hand into the lunch box and grab lunch bag that belong to someone else because I didn't want the biscuit lunch my mother had made for me. I used to think that all of the other children in my class had a much better lunch than the one I had. There was always someone at one of the last tables called after me who was left with my lunch, and the unfortunate child would start to cry because someone had taken his or her lunch bag. The child knew that the lunch bag they brought to school didn't have a biscuit with syrup in it. Because there were no names written on the lunch bags for identification, our teacher was puzzled. I played this game until the teacher got wise to my tricks. To eliminate this problem, our teacher instructed all of the children I our class to have their parents write their names on their lunch bags for identification my grabbing the wrong lunch bag days were over. However, once the children got a taste of my syrup and biscuit sandwich, they were always willing trade their lunch for mine on the playground before we entered the classroom. My recollection of the second and third grade was in Mr. Henry's class. He was a very neat man who dressed in a brown three-piece wool suit. He was very strict and liked to administer punishment on little boys. Mr. Henry took pleasure in kicking little boys in the butt with his knee or a paddle on your buttocks in the cloakroom. He would sometimes have you drop your pants and spank you on your rear end, and dare you to tell your parents. Today, that would be called child molestation or sexual abuse. When I think of all the things he did to us, I believe he was a sexual predator because he loved to inflict pain on little boys. He was the playground monitor, and would booth you or grab you rear end if he caught you coming out of the woods, violating any one of the playground rules, or if you were late returning from recess or because you had to walk home for lunch. All the little boys at Garfield feared him. I remember one little boy's father came to the school and beat up Mr. Henry because of what he did to his son. I was always too scared to tell my parents for fear of getting a whipping. A child accusing an adult was always questionable, unless there was physical evidence to support your statement. If you didn't have the support of physical evidence back in those days, the word of an adult over a child's allegations was never questioned. The backward thinking of our parents in those days traumatized the minds of many children. Numerous children were victims of incest and child abuse that went unnoticed, because most adults did not believe to words of a child when they accused an adult of child molestation or physical abuse. Because of the traumatic experiences that happened to me at the age of nine, I blocked it out of my mind throughout my child hood years and blacked out my attendance at Anita Turner Elementary School. I do not remember my attendance in the fourth through the sixth grades. I do remember graduating from the sixth grade in 1952 and being promoted to attend the seventh grade at the new Fredrick Douglass Junior High school. I do remember how I had to shuffle my feet across the stage without lifting my shoes off the floor, for fear that the children standing behind me would see the holes in the bottom of my shoes and began to laugh and make fun of me and the holes in my shoes. My shoes were so worn out that the soles had come loose from stitches that hold the bottom sole of the shoe to the top of the shoe. When the stitches wore out the sole would flap like a lip when you walked. When I graduated from Turner Elementary School in 1953, I made a promise to myself that if I every got up on my feet and got a job, I would always buy and wear only the best of shoes and clothes and by the grace of God and his blessing I have been able to keep that promise.

SODOMIZE ME

When I was nine years old my friend Tommy Jordan and I got up early one morning to steal some pears from Mr. Mac's pear tree next to his vegetable garden. As planned, Tommy met me at the rear of my house. We went down to the chain link fence down by the little stream that ran under the fence on to Mr. Mac's property. Just before the rooster crowed at break of day, we climbed the back fence that separated our back yard and Mr. Mac's farm, and began to fill our cloth bags with moist pears covered with the dew that had fallen on the ground the night before. Just as we had gathered most of the pears, we looked up and saw two teen age boys running towards us. Tommy and I were so scared that we didn't know what to do. We pleaded with them not to beat us up for stealing the pears out of Mr. Mac's garden. They grabbed us by the arms and took us into Mr. Mac's house. We thought they were going to turn us in to Mr. Mac, but they had something else on their minds. When they got us into the farmhouse, they pushed us on the bed and pulled down our short pants and began to sodomize both of us. It was such a horrible experience. I was traumatized by the incident, and blocked it out of my mind for more than 20 years of my life. To add to that traumatic incident, it seems as thought I was always the target of the school bullies or the butt of someone's joke. The second and third floors of Anita Turner Elementary School were temporary class rooms for the seventh to ninth grade junior high school students awaiting the opening of the newly constructed Fredrick Douglass Junior High School. I was always singled out for some reason or another or maybe just because the clothes I wore were tattered and soiled. To add to my dilemma I had a 'mama hair cut' or a bald head. A mama cut was a hair cut your mother gave to you with a set of hand-operated clippers. The hair clippers blades were very dull and most of your hair was pulled out instead of being cut. At the end of the hair cut experience I would have so many patches in your hair the only solution to correct the mama cut was to have all the hair cut off your head. A bald head when I was a youngster was made fun of and not acceptable when I was growing up. If you had a bald head almost everybody would say you look like little Henry in the newspaper cartoon. I seem although everybody wanted to slap your bald head and make fun of you. I believe that is the reason why I always wear a hat to this day. The bullies at school would have a field day with my head. They used to grab me by the left arm with their left hand, with their right hand about mid-way up my back, and walk me in front of all the school kids (mainly by the girls) and tell me to look up at the moon. When I looked up into the air, the bully would take the hand that he had placed on my back and bring it up with such force, slapping the back of my head so hard that it would slam my chin into my chest. They would do this on a daily basis. I would try to hide, but they would always fine me. The most humiliating part was that they would slap my bald head in front of the teenage girls; they thought slapping was funny, and they would laugh hysterically and tell the bullies to do it again. For approximately 20 to 30 years, I blocked out the traumatic bullying experience I had at Turner Elementary School, and the devastating act that happened to me in Mr. Mac's house. In my adult life, I have read several newspaper article and watch several television talk shows regarding abused children who had blocked out child molestation, incest or a child hood traumatic experience that happen to them during their adolescent years. The tragedy is when those horrible experiences reappear in your adult life. The tragic experience I had reappeared when I was home on leave from the Air Force in the fall of 1986. I was on a bus riding through my old neighborhood, when one of the teenagers who had assaulted me got on the bus. I had a flashback of the whole incident. I remembered the teenager's name and in a split moment in anger I called it out. "Tinaman!!!!!" He turned around and looked at me, and wondered in his mind how I knew his name. My brain began to work overtime putting all the pieces together. I was enraged and angry at what he had done to me and my friend. My only thought at that time was how can I destroy this person for what he did to me and Tommy. In 1986 at this time I use to carry a 9-mm Spanish Lager in the breast pocket of my special made leather coat. It was all clear I was contemplating confronting him when he got off the bus and possibly killing him. When I then looked up to monitor his activity and at what bus stop he would get off at he was not on the bus. I got off the bus and ran as fast as I could to see if he got off the bus at any of the previous stops. I believe in my heart if I could have found him I would have blown his brains out of his head. However, God's had a different plan and removed the man from my presence, because God saw my thoughts and knew in my heart that I was not a murderer God save me from one of the ten commandment in the Holy Bible "Thou Shall Not Kill" I saw the fear on the man's face when I called out his name. He said nothing. He was a shell of a man, and looked very sickly, as though he was afflicted with some type of incurable disease. I know that if I were to meet Tinaman today, I would do nothing to harm him. I would pray for him, because I know deep down in my heart God was with both of us at that time of my flashback. Maybe Tinaman had repented to God, and to take his life would have been a violation of one the ten commandments of my faith: "Thou Shall Not kill" and "Love your Neighbor as you Love Yourself". Since that incident, I have asked God to forgive me for the sin of thought, because in my mind I had already killed Tinaman. If you have an experience similar to mine, please seek help from an advocacy group or your God. By no means should you try to be the judge and jury on such a serious matter; forgive and move on with your life, because the stress is not worth it. In time, justice will prevail. "Vengeance is mine said the Lord"

KILLER HILL

Washington D. C. had some heavy snow storms during the winter months in my adolescent years. The snow storm would last for two or three days. The District Government would close all the schools in the area, because a snow storm could virtually cripple the city roads. After the snow began to melt, the street and sidewalks would freeze to solid ice, and it was dangerous for anyone to walk or drive on it. It always appeared that the Public Works Department was never prepared to handle a snow storm of any magnitude. We would always listen to WTOP radio station for the latest news and update on the schools opening and closing. The heaviest snow storms would drop around three or four feet of crystal-clear white snow. The snow would sometimes turn to sleet, a form of falling icy water. This sleet would stick to the trees and accumulate on the limbs until they could no longer hold the weight of the snow, so the limbs would sometimes break and destroy anything below it. I have seen a whole tree split down the middle because one side was saturated with sleet. The snow was like a magnet: for some reason it has a power that seems to draw children to it. They always want to play in the beautiful white stuff, even though you get wet and the snow freezes our fingers in the old socks we used to ware for gloves on our hands. My grandmother Hattie had a saying she used to say that the snow was God's way of cleaning the earth of all impurities and disease. This really made sense to me, because after a snow storm, the air would be crystal-clear and had such a fresh clean smell. After a major snow storm, all the children in our neighborhood wanted to do build Frosty the snow man. The competition was on: to see who could build the biggest and best looking snow man, fort or igloo in the neighborhood. Families from all over the neighborhood would take their evening strolls throughout the neighborhood to view and select the best snow creations. I was not artistic and could never build a snow man or figure that even resembled Frosty the Snowman. My snowmen were not rounded and shaped like a snowman. They were fat, flat, dirty and out-of-shape. My creation of a snowman didn't get many visitors. Once the snow was packed to the ground and the sun had melted it, and the low temperature in the air made the snow hard. Now was the time to wax the runner blades on our sled and go for a ride down Killer Hill. We called it Killer Hill because several children I remember road their sled down the wrong side of killer hill leading into the main road and they were either injured or killed by moving vehicles when their sleds went out into the street. Killer Hill was located in the Parkland Apartments subdivisions, adjacent to the chain link fence that separated the Parkland apartments from Camp Simms Army Depot. Killer Hill was a forty-degree down hill slope that leveled off for about six feet and then continued for another fifteen to twenty yards. As you approached the apartment buildings at the end of the sled run, who ever was riding the sled had to navigate between the openings of the two buildings. If you failed to navigate the sled as you approached the buildings, or your sled veered off track as you headed down hill, you had only one choice roll off the sled to avoid crashing head on into one of the buildings. The opening between the buildings was about twenty to forty-five feet. The path we used on the hill was very dangerous, but a lot of fun if you stayed on the sled path. I always had a good run and never once got hurt. If, your sled veered off the sled path, you when riding our sled down hill , you had to roll off the sled into the deep snow and your day for sled riding was over because you would be saturated with snow from your head to the bottom of your feet. If you escaped with a few cuts and bruises, you were lucky because most of the children who crashed into the bricks of the apartment building thought they could stop themselves by stretching out their arm and hands while traveling at 35 to 50 miles per hour. Several of the children who crashed into the building received broken arms, fingers, hands, and brain concussions. The second option was to try and get back on the sled path and continue the run between the apartment buildings. This wasn't a good option, because of the danger of crashing into one of the buildings. I remember one particular day we were all in one apartment building at the top of the hill at the beginning of our sled run. We were in the warm hallway in the apartment building trying to warm up our cold hands and toes. My brother Aubrey ran into the apartment building and told us that my friend Tooth's brother, Russell, had taken one of the sleds and was on his way to the sled path down Killer Hill. We ran out of the building, hoping to catch Russell and stop him. We were too late. We saw Russell running toward the sled path and watch him flopped onto the sled at top speed down Killer Hill. Russell was not on the regular sled path that went between the two apartment buildings. He veered off the track, and was headed straight for one of the buildings. We began to scream at the top of our voices, trying to get Russell to roll of the sled. Apparently Russell did not hear us, and continued towards the apartment buildings with one his arms straight out in front of his head with the intention of trying to stop himself from crashing into the apartment buildings. In a split second we heard a loud cracking sound. Russell had crashed into the buildings, and was standing on his feet wandering around in a circle as though he was drunk. When we finally got to the bottom of the hill, the first words he uttered, after seeing his brother Tooth, were," Tooth, am I dead? Am I dead?" Russell collapsed on the ground with a big lump on his forehead and a broken arm. It was very cold back in those days, and we didn't have adequate clothes for the inclement weather. We would put on as many pair of socks as we could, and put on our rubber boots. We would put on long underwear and two pairs of pants. Almost everybody had a mackinaw: a 100% heavy wool coat that was handed down through the families. We would put on two or three mismatched socks for gloves. Our snow playing clothes would last about two hours before we were soaking wet from head to toe. We always knew it was time to quit riding our sleds or playing in the snow. The first indication was that your hands and toes would be numb, and so cold that all you could do was cry all the way home. Mom would run cold water on our cold hands and rub them with her warm hands until our hands were warm again. After warming up we were ready to go back out side to play in the snow once again and have some more fun. We would build snow forts and have snowball fights. Snow in the winter always reminded me that Christmas season was approaching fast. Our parents use to say "Christmas is just around the corner". When I heard that saying, I was always looking and trying to find the corner they were talking about.

CHARLIE SLED RIDE;

Even though the winter was very cold, it was the fun season in Washington D.C. I remember after the snow fall, we use to go slay riding on a hill that crossed a little creak directly behind our house. Most of the boys from our circle would go for a sled ride on the hill. We would run and flop on our sleds and hid down the little hill and try to jump our sleds across to the other side of the creak. I remember the day when Charlie Stewart tried to jump the creak and the front of his sled and got stuck in the bank on the other side of the creak. Because Charlie did not lift his sled up high enough during his jump, his sled got stuck in the creak bank and his body kept going forward and the bottom set of his teeth hit the bank and dislocated his jaw bone. We thought Charlie look funny because he could not close his mouth. When we were children we would laugh at anything funny. We laugh at Charlie because his face looked funny we were not aware of the seriousness of Charlie's injuries.

ATLANTIC CITY;

After the school year was over in June of each year we began our summer vacation. Because we were poor we did not have much to do on our vacation and we didn't have a swimming pool in our neighborhood, and there were not many places we could visit or go to for recreation except for the mall on the grounds between the US Capital and the Washington Monument. Several of my friends were selected by the state or church to attend two weeks of summer camp. I was never lucky enough to be selected for anything or to go anywhere for fun and enjoyment. To break up the monopoly, my dad would take us for a ride in his company truck. The United Publishing Company allowed my dad to use their truck for his personal transportation after he completed his evening deliveries. The truck was well insulated with two doors at the rear of the truck. Each door was approximately ten inches thick, with locking handles on each door. Dad would lock us in the truck when we were going on a trip. On many occasions, we were locked in the truck with no fresh air for two or three hours. We did not know that we were in danger of suffocating. However, we would do anything to go on a trip with Dad. Atlantic City trip; In July of each year, my grandmother's Church would sponsor a bus trip to Atlantic City. I could not wait for that day. In preparation for the trip, my grandmother (Hattie Hodge) would normally take me and my older sister Consuella on a shopping trip down town to the Hecht's Company or the Murphy's 5 & 10 cent store to shop for clothes for us to wear on the Atlantic City bus trip,. On this one particular occasion, my grandmother took my sister shopping and brought her all kinds of different clothes. After shopping with Consuella granny told me that she was low on money, and would have to take me shopping at the Salvation Army Thrift Store to buy me some used clothes to wear on the trip. I was very depressed for the first time in my life, and made my first major decision. I told my grandmother that I didn't think what she did was fair spending all of her money on my sister Consuella and wanting to take me to the Thrift Store to buy me use clothing. I told her that I was not going to Atlantic City with her that year and I also called her a big fat red tomato. She was sharked and very upset with me because I called her a bad name. Granny held what I said to he against me for 14 years or until I was 22 years old. The lesson I learned from that experience was to always respect your elders and never call them name even though you are mad as hell. I believe a thrift store curse was levied on me from that day to the present, because, I do most of my major shopping at thrift stores all over the world. I have found some of the greatest bargains and deals in thrift stores and yard sales. I learned from my mother that a thrift store is a good place to find some of the most interesting things, and some of the best and most expensive used clothing and furniture.

THE FREDERICK DOUGLASS RECREATION CENTER

The Frederick Douglass Recreation Center was located on top of the hill in our housing development, on the corner of Alabama Avenue and Stanton Terrace. The Center was the only place we could go for recreation. In the summer, the Center offered a day camp. It only had limited equipment for us to play with: two or three basketball courts with hoops without nets, one broken checker board like a pool table, checkers, crayons and paper. We always looked forward to summer camp, because they would have arts and crafts. We could make key chains and necklaces out of plastic strips. I was always good at arts and crafts; they were my favorite pastime. I was always interested in making or repairing things. I used to build children's lawn chairs out of wooden cantaloupe boxes and sell them. Every Friday night during the summer, the Frederick Douglass Center would have a dance contest. Teenagers from all over town would come to the recreation center to show off their dancing talents. The best dance couple could win the best dancer trophy and two tickets to the Howard Theater. The winners were heroes to us, and everybody wanted to dance just like them. They were the talk of the neighborhood—they set the dress style. I remember one year, one of the dancers had a split in the bottom of his pants legs with an added piece of colored cloth in between the splits. We call them bell bottoms today. All the boys in the 'hood wanted to have an extra piece of cloth material sewed on the sides of their pants legs. My sister Consuella was one of the best dancers in town. All the male dancers would try their turn at swing dancing or doing the jitterbug with her. She was good and never missed a step or turn when they tried to fool her. You couldn't fool my sister—she was a natural swinger. She learned her dancing from the parties we had at our house every Friday and Saturday night in our kitchen. We learned to do all the new dances there. I wasn't a bad dancer myself. I could really shake a leg, and all the young girls in the neighborhood wanted to dance with me. I did not want to participate in the contest for fear of being beaten up by jealous onlookers. I was afraid to dance with anybody except my sister Consuella. The summer nights were very hot and humid. We would get soaking wet all over, and would continue to dance to the music. The mosquitoes would have a field day feasting on our hot and sweaty bodies. The chiggers had their day too, if you stood or danced on the dirt. Back in those days we didn't have insect repellant. The only way to avoid being attacked by insects was to be stinky, and I fell in that category because I did not like to take a bath. The dance at the center was where everybody came to show off their talents. The recreation center was not a safe place because numerous dangerous gangs came from all over the city. Just about everything went on in the dark areas of the recreation center. Teenagers drank beer, wine and whiskey, smoked cigarettes and marijuana and so of the teenager would have sex in the dark areas of the recreation field behind the basket ball courts. I was a loner and always went to the dance alone, looking for a girlfriend. I was shy and was always waiting for a girl to come up to me and ask me if I wanted to be her boyfriend. I was never lucky enough to find a girlfriend, because, I didn't have nice clothes to wear. In our culture, clothes played an important part in a man's life when it came to getting a girlfriend. There was always a fist fight over some girl after the dance, or between some rival gang who came from another part of town. Officer Goodoff (the local police officer) would try to prevent fights or break up any confrontation at the Center, and send everybody home. When Officer Goodoff spoke, you reacted or suffered a swift kick in the butt, or he would hit you with his Billy stick if you did not follow his directions or you tried to talk back to him. The dance was always a topic of conversation for several weeks or until the next dance.

DAVE'S SUPERMARKET

Dave's supermarket was the only grocery store in our neighborhood. There were other stores and shopping centers close by, but we couldn't go in the white neighborhood to shop, so they were off-limits to blacks. Because most of the families were poor, and were short on money by mid-week, almost all the families in the neighborhood had a charge account at Dave's. He would exploit everybody. He took advantage of those who were poor and considered un-educated. The price on all of Dave's groceries was doubled in price when you purchased items on credit. Dave was a cheater he would always add additional items to your monthly bill list. Dave did not give you a register receipt for the groceries you purchased. Dave would rely on you forgetting what items you had purchased during the month. Often, our parents would send one of their older children to the store with a list of items to be purchase on credit. Dave would let us shop for the groceries it and would add additional items to his credit book after we had checked out. I can remember watching Dave taking his left finger and thumb and to hold the scale down to add additional pound or ounces to scaleable meat or vegetable items he was weighing. Because Dave's store was the only grocery store on our side of town that offered our parents credit account for groceries, our parents were force to patronize Dave's Grocery Store. If our parents challenge Dave's or disagreed with his book keepings practices he would revoke their credit account. I truly believe during the segregation period in the 1950s and 60s most white thought that black people were dumb or uneducated because they were poor. However, what they didn't know was we have a rich background. We are descended from African Kings, Emperors and Potentates. Most blacks have a good heart and we were taught by our parents to love everybody and trust in God for our strength. Our grandfathers took a lot of abuse for us. They had to hold their piece and let the Lord fight their battle. Rising up would only mean the genocide of our race. They saw what happen to the Indians when they rebelled against the white Anglo Saxons. Their only hope was to pray for that one day when his grandchild's grandchild could be free of discrimination and be accepted to attend college of their choice and one day be elected to one of the highest posts in our government and maybe in the future the office of the president of the United States. Some of us have fulfilled their dreams. No matter how bad I was treated, I was taught by my parents never to practice an eye for an eye or a tooth for a tooth. Because Dave's was so mean and charge outrageous prices for everything. There were a lot of people who was stealing from Dave's store on a daily basis. I heard the words leach and blood sucker mention concerning people coming into our neighborhood sucking it dry and never invested a penny back in the neighborhood. Dave was that kind of person. He took and stole from everybody who patronized his store. When I was working in Dave's meat department, Dave noticed that he was losing a lot of money out of the meat department's account. Each week after inventory we couldn't balance the account. We could not account for large items such as whole and half hams, chickens, beef round, and pork roast. Dave accused us of stealing his meat. Dave had an intercom system installed in the store for communicating from the meat department to the checkout counter where Dave operated the cash register. He instructed us to call him every time someone purchased a large weighted item from the meat department.

I remember on this one particular day, a neighbor lady named Ms Oteah Long was shopping for groceries in Dave's store. She had one of the biggest families in the projects dwelling. Mr. And Mrs. Earnest Long had 12 children and they all lived in a two-bedroom dwelling. Ms Oteah was doing her regular shopping, and when she got to the meat department she ordered a 15-pound ham. We wrapped it in brown butcher's paper and gave it to her, and she continued to shop throughout the store. I contacted Dave on the intercom and told him that Ms Oteah had just picked up a 15-pound ham. When Ms Oteah got to the checkout counter, the ham was missing from her shopping cart. Dave asked her where the ham was. Ms Oteah said she didn't have a ham, and start to talk in a loud voice. Dave told her to look out the window of the exit door. Through the window you could see a police scout car parked across the street adjacent to the store with Officer Goodoff sitting in it. Dave told Ms Oteah to give up the ham or he would call Officer Goodoff to search her and if he found the ham he would have her locked up. She continued to deny that she had the ham. Dave told her that if she didn't do some jumping jacks for him, he would bring in the law. Ms Oteah weighed about 300 pounds. She did one jumping jack and the ham, which she had hidden between her thighs under her long dress, fell to the floor. Dave told her to pick up that stinky ham and get the hell out of his store. All the children thought Dave was a good man until that tragic day when he scattered a box of Exlax on the ground. Every day about 12:30, all the black school children would gather in front of Dave's store. He would come out of his store and throw about 80 or 100 pieces of candy corns in the air like he was feeding hungry chickens. All the kids would scramble for the candy. They would kick and scratch, trying to get a piece of candy. Dave seemed to enjoy seeing the little black children act like animals. On this particular day, Dave threw out about 200 sample packages of Exlaxs We didn't have to do much scrambling that day, because there were so many packages available on the ground. All the children tried to fill up their pockets. After returning to school from lunch, everything was normal. About 1:30, all hell broke loose in the school. Almost all the children who had eaten the Exlax had to go to the restroom at the same time. Some of the children had their intestines hanging out. Almost all of the children had defecated in their under-garments. About 75% of the children in the school were sick with diarrhea that day. Parents who had a few dollars filed a law suit against Dave's Super Market and won their case, however, my family was not included in the law suit and we didn't get anything. I believe my family was excluded because we were poor. Because of the shelter my parents provided for us, we thought that we were rich when we were very poor, we never knew that we were discriminated against or what discrimination was, because our parents did a good job of hiding discrimination from us. We were always taken to black theaters, restaurants, parks and beaches. Both of my parents had good hearts. They did not believe in an eye for an eye. My Parents taught me to love everybody as God so loved this world". I have practice those saying all my life and J have been truly blessed by God.

GARDEN TEA SHOPPE

I will never forget working at the Garden Tea Shoppe, an exclusive restaurant for the rich people in uptown Washington D.C. My dad had a part-time job working as a busboy at the Garden Tea Shoppe on Saturdays and Sundays. His job was to clear all the china and food off the tables after the customers had finish dining. We would always eat well on those weekends when dad worked at the Garden Tea Shoppe. My brothers and sisters looked forward to dad bringing home the poppy seed buttered rolls, breads, French pastries, petit fours, slices of cakes and pies. On specials when he worked a banquet dad would bring home pieces of steak, chicken and a variety of European cuisine. I use to work as a dishwasher at the Shoppe; however, because I was underage, the owner not put me on the payroll. He would give my dad the money I earned I was always glad to be able to work at the Garden Tea Shoppe mainly because I was able to experience eating many different kinds of gourmet foods, cakes and pies. Dad would call me to help him when the dishwasher didn't show up for work, or when they needed help with a large party. I would ride the Navy Yard Bus (the B-6) and transfer to the 92 Calvert Street Bridge street car that took me to 18th and Columbia road North West Washington D.C. where the Garden Tea Shoppe was located. The customers who patronized the Garden Tea Shoppe was mostly rich white people from the upper-class neighborhoods; doctors, lawyers and politicians. Because of the segregation laws, most of the restaurants downtown did not cater to black patrons. We had a few black and Chinese restaurants around town where we could get a good meal. We had numerous chicken, seafood and barbecue restaurants and carryout shops located all over town and in our neighborhoods. There was Liquor stores on almost every corner in our neighborhood. The Jim Crow laws that were in affect during that period of time prohibited blacks from sitting down and eating in white restaurants or at fast food counters in any of the drug or department stores that served prepare food. When I was growing up you taught not to waste food or throw good food away. It seemed as thought all the rich customers who ate at the Garden Tea Shoppe did not understand the war time etiquettes we were taught by our parents to eat everything on your plate and you could not throw away anything, because there were children in Japan and other countries overseas starving. The Garden Tea Shoppe customers would always leave untouched food items on their plates. Dad instructed me to save all the meat, potatoes, and pastry that had not been eaten. At the end of the working day, we would have saved enough food to feed our whole family of five for two or three days. Mom would always share the spoils from the Tea Shoppe with our neighbors. Those were the good old days. My favorite piece of pastry was the French petit four with the pink and white cream icing, and the bear claws laced with walnuts and brown filling inside the bun that taste like a mixture of plums and apple butter.

THE FIGHT;

It was Friday afternoon. on my way home from school while getting off the W-6 Garfield Loop bus at Stanton Road and Bruce Place, I noticed a large crowd of teenagers surrounding two young boys about 15 yards from the bus stop. I was curious and ventured over to the crowd to see what the commotion was all about. There were approximately 10 to 15 bullies surrounding the two young boys and attacking them. Later I found out that the fight started when one of the bullies asked Morris for a cigarette, and he refused to give him one, and told him to buy his own. I notice that the bullies were attacking them from all sides, using every dirty tactic they could think of. One of the bullies would pretending to be taunting one of the young teenagers, Morris, while the other bullies would attack him from the rear. The mob leader's name was Buckley Fields, and he was from the Berry Farms Project area. While looking at the odds, I thought the fight was very unfair; I joined the two brothers to even up the odds. Morris and I teamed up to keep the bullies from attacking Willie from behind. Willie was a strong country boy who had a powerful right hook that was knocking the bullies out one by one. We ended up beating all 10 to 15 of the bullies. The crowd of teenagers was mad because we won the fight. They joined our enemies and began to attack us also. We had to fight the crowd of both girls and boys, for about twenty more minutes or until my sister Dale ran to my house and told my mother that I was in a fight with a crowd of teenagers at the bus stop. My mother ran up to the corner and stopped the fight. I really do not know what had come over me on that day. I was never a violent person nor would I interfere into someone else's business. I was a loner and usually minded my own business. When I saw how the odds were stacked against the two young boys, I reacted without thinking, and have never regret doing what I did that day. That night a gang of teenagers were congregating in the parking lot in front of Ms. Slade's Restaurant making their plans to attack Willie's house. We heard that the crowd was going to have another fight that night at Willie's House. They gathered in the open field at the back of Willie's house. Willie and I were setting in at the kitchen table talking with his mother about the incident that happen earlier that day, when a large rock came crashing through the kitchen window and landed on the kitchen table where we were eating. Willie and I went outside to see what had happen. When we got outside we saw a large mob of about 50 to 100 teenagers congregated in the alley and in the open field in the rear of his house. They were throwing large rocks at us and calling us names. Willie's mother came outside to tell the crowd to go away, when she was hit in the head with a brick. We got her back into the house. We came back outside and took out our sling shots and began to sling large rocks into the crowd. We were hitting them and knocking them down like flies, and they began to take cover and throwing a barrage of rocks at us that landed all up against Willie's mother's house. Willie's Brother Herbert arrived home from work just in time and heard the commotion in the back yard he got his double-barreled shotgun and shot a warning shot above the mob's head dispersing them. From that day, Willie Boy and I became best friends for life. Willie fell in love with my sister Dale and they got married and had two beautiful girls. Willie and I have been bonded friends every since that day we met at the fight.

A SCARY MOMENT

One cold rainy morning while walking to school with my friends, we stopped at the drug store to buy a piece of penny candy. I didn't have a penny, but went in the store anyway and stood in line. The candy display was in line with the check-out counter. We were Line up alongside the candy, and you could choose the pieces you wanted while standing in line. I had on a Maconog coat and a pair of wool knickers with argons socks. As I moved past the candy display, I picked up several packages of Lifesavers, butterscotch's and some candy bars. I slipped them in my knickers pocket as I moved forward, and then I picked up a Clark bar and a Baby Ruth. That wasn't enough. I picked up a pack of Juicy Fruit chewing gum, three jaw breakers, two Mary James, four squirrel nuts, two B.B. Bats and five packs of KIXs. When I arrived at the check-out counter, I told Doc that I didn't want anything, but that I was with my friend. One of Doc's workers grabbed me by the arm and told Doc that he saw me put some candy in my pocket. I told Doc that I didn't steal anything. I was lying and was so scared; I began to sweat profusely and was shaking nervously. I knew that I was headed for Blue Plains Boys' Home, where I would be attacked by Puggy Green, the big guy who plugs little boys in the butt. Doc grabbed me and patted both of my pockets, and found nothing. He told me to get the hell out of his store and not come back into the store unless I was going to buy something. As I continued my journey to school, I went under the Alabama Avenue Street Bridge to see what happened to the candy I put in my pockets. I was not aware that I had a hole in my knickers pocket, and each time I put a piece of candy in my pocket, it just slipped through the hole and lodged in the knee gathering of my knickers. I learned a lesson that day about stealing, but it wasn't very long before I was at it again.

I began stealing money from out of my dad's change fund on his dresser. I used to take a nickel or a dime from his dresser, and I thought for sure that he wouldn't miss it. I graduated from taking the nickels to stealing his half-dollars. I thought Dad didn't know what was going on until I got up early this one morning and slip into his bedroom to take some more change from his dresser. I thought Dad was asleep, but he was lying there watching me, and he let me go through my routine of stealing and hiding the money in my room, then let me go back to sleep. When Dad was ready to go to work, he told Mom that he was missing some money. He called me into his room and asked me if I had seen any of his money. I said "No "but said that I would try to help him find it. I was looking in his closet, in his work shoes under his bed, and in mama's hat-box. Dad said "Let's look in your bedroom." He took me by the arm to my bedroom and told me to look under my bed. I looked under the bed and saw nothing. He said "Look under the slats and he raised the mattress", and the money was there. I was embarrassed, scared and did not know what to do or say. Dad told me to take off my clothes because he was going to teach me not to steal. That whipping dad put on me that day taught me a very important lesson. Since that day I have never stole anything. I believe in working for what you want; because, there is a price you have to pay for stealing.

FRIDAY NIGHT FISH FRY

On Friday our whole family looked forward with anticipation to the Friday night fish fry at our house. All the kids in the neighborhood would congregate at our house, waiting for Dad and Uncle John to come home to begin the party. Uncle John would bring my mother fresh caught fish from one of the fish boats or stands at the wharf in Southwest Washington D.C. Granny would pull out her penny purse and challenge us to one of her favorite card games: pity pat, tunk or coon can. She would try and win all the loose change we had in our pockets. Most of our friends in the 'hood would bring their 45-inch records to our house. Somebody would always have the number one hit for that week. As soon as the sun went down, we would put a red or blue light bulb in the lamp and turn on the music. It was Eddie's rule that if you had a girlfriend or boyfriend, you had to dance with them on the first slow jam. The summertime in Washington was very hot and muggy, and we would dance all night if they let us. After a few hours of fast jitterbugging and slow dancing we called it the RUB, but today they call it dirty dancing), in the hot house our body were soaking wet from perspiration. The smell of male and female hormones was all through the house. Uncle John would show up between 6:30 and 7 o'clock and the singing would begin. Uncle John would pull out his Jews harp and ukulele, and begin to sing the song "Five foot two, eyes are blue". We would all join in the sing-along. Mr. George, one of my dad's co-workers, would come over and bring a pint of gin and case of beer. Mom and Granny would start cooking the fish, and would fry a pan of potatoes and cabbage. Mom would also make a big pot of spaghetti with hamburger meat. They would cook enough food for everybody in the house. Uncle John would get so drunk; I don't know how he ever got home. I remember Uncle John's wife, because she never liked us and was always sad. Uncle John and his wife Liz was always fighting or arguing about something when ever my sister Consuella and I visited their house. Almost every Sunday afternoon after we came home from church, Mom would give Tike (my oldest sister) a dollar to buy a bus pass for dad's bus transportation to and from work. Tyke would purchase the bus pass and we would ride all over town for free and visit our relatives. We would visit my Uncle John's house first. His wife had a bad disposition and she seems to be sad all the time. Her actions and demeanor was cold and snotty towards my sister and me because we were poor and lived in the project dwelling. Uncle John always treated us with the utmost respect and never once looked down on us because of the condition our family was in. Uncle John was always there for my mother and dad to lend a helping hand when needed. He would always visit our house at lease once or twice a week. He was crazy about his sister (my mother) and treated her like a queen. He called mom by the nickname he gave her Sally, and my dad by his nickname Saddle low. My dad and my Uncle John were best of friends until the day he died. Uncle John, Dad and Mr. George would drink gin and grapefruit juice on Friday night and play checkers or coon-can until the early hours of Saturday morning. Uncle John was the song leader and would sing songs like 'Mack the Knife', 'Won't You Come Home Bill Bailey' It aint necessary so and many others. All the songs would end up with the same lines; "MAMA CAUSE I LOVE YOU SO AND I WANT YOU TO KNOW THAT I'M IN LOVE WITH YOU. BOB DUBE DUBE DOP DO DAY YEH!!!" I loved my

Uncle John because he was genuine and real. He had such an impact on my life. I try each and every day to emulate the love he showed me, and spread that love to anyone I come in contact with. He was a great teacher and didn't know it. Uncle John had a saying: "He was a poet and didn't know it". We always anticipated a visit to Uncle John's house because we new that he would have some goodies for us to eat. He would top it off by letting us reach our little hands into his gallon pickle jar full of pennies and take all the pennies our two little hands could hold. We thought we were rich as millionaires on that day with our pockets full of pennies. On our way home, would stop at the Navy Yard Bakery and buy a nickel slice of ginger bread covered with chocolate icing with raisins inside. O that day we thought we were in hog heaven.

SUNDAY BUS RIDE AND VISITS

On Sunday after church my mother would give Consuella one dollar to buy a bus pass. On Sundays, three children plus the pass-holder could ride the bus all day for free. We would visit all of our relatives on that day. We would catch the W-6 bus that took us to the Navy Yard and we would get a transfer and catch the 92 Street car bound for the Calvert Street Bridge. We would ride to 8th and H street N.E., get off the street car and catch the bus to the Lafayette Square bus, and get off at Third and H street N. E. at the bus stop by the Little Sister of the Poor Convent. We would visit my cousins Estelle, Chink, Marie and Johnnie. Estelle always had some government food and two or three watermelons. She always had some leftover cornbread, which was good, cold or hot, with King Syrup on it. Estelle would give you anything to eat, but she wouldn't give you a penny if you asked for it. She was always hungry for money. She would always give Mom anything she asked for. Estelle had a genuine love for children, and was a true Catholic and attended church every Sunday. You had to remember that when eating food in Estelle's house, you had to eat fast, because your meal could be sold to someone at anytime. I remember one Friday evening, all of the construction workers who boarded in Estelle's house showed up. She would provide them with dinner and collect their rent. Estelle also boot-legged whiskey and she would provide all the renters with booze throughout the week-end. Come Monday morning, Estelle would have all their money and they would be in debt to Estelle. If we were eating, and one of the workers came into the house and was hungry for something to eats, Estelle would pull the plate from in front of us, spruce it up and sell it to one of the workers. We had to eat a bowl of dry cereal with Carnation canned milk. After the visit to Estelle, we traveled on the bus and street car to the Navy Yard in South East, and stopped at Aunt Virginia's and the Digg's House. We could hear music and cussing as we approached their little apartment in the basement. Her house was very dimly lit with a 25-watt light bulb. All the furniture was tattered and ripped and soil, with cotton falling out of the pillows. The kitchen table was full of soiled dishes, with roaches crawling everywhere. The smell of stale wine and beer was throughout the house. Empty beer cans and bottles were in every corner on the floor. Virginia always had one or two babies in her apartment. It appeared the babies' diapers had not been changed since the day before, and the babies smelled of sour milk, urine and stinky feces. Underneath the filth and stench in the apartment, Virginia had a heart of gold, and the love she gave us overpowered the condition in which she was living in. Her love made us feel like we were royalty in a queen's palace. When we left Virginia's apartment, we went across the street to Uncle Robert's house. The first thing you saw when his wife opened the apartment door was a giant leather chair with a six-foot back with Uncle Robert sitting in the middle of the chair. The apartment was always dim, with just a little sun light peeping through the shade on the window. Every step across the wooden floor was heard. As we approached him, he would say in a deep voice "COME HERE!!!" I thought he sounded like the giant in 'Jack and the bean stalk'. I was always scared when I entered his house, and couldn't wait to leave. We had to sit on his knee and answer his questions. He never gave us anything but fear. We left his house and walked two blocks to Uncle John's house, and had a good time. After Uncle

John's, we went another block to Grandpa Charlie's red house with the four-seat swing covered with grapevines. Grandpa was a good old man. He was not educated. He could not read or write, and for some reason he disliked my mother. Grandpa was well off—he had money but he couldn't count it. He would always give my sister Consuella and me a dime and a piece of Ms. Lidded Belle's pound cake. I believe he thought he was Mr. Rocker fellow. You had to be watchful how you talked in his house, because if you said something good about Mom or my Grandma Hattie, he would put us out and wouldn't give us anything. The lady who lived with Grandpa was named Miss Lidded Belle. She made some of the best-tasting pound cakes. They were about 6 to 8 inches thick. She used to sell them to the white folks. After Grandpa's house, we would go around the corner to our Grandma Hattie's house. She would be nice to us. We had to go see great grandma, she was always sick in the bedroom. Aunt Moore, Granny's sister, lived there also. She was the cook of the house. I can't remember anything significant that happened at Granny's house. I do remember how she would take Counsuella into her bedroom and give her ten cents, and then she would come out and make like she didn't have any money, and give me her last three pennies. Tyke would always split the dime with me that granny had given her. Tyke was always protective and good to me. She would never let anybody abuse or hurt me. Her love extends beyond the grave. I remember her love and goodness and I continue love her even though she is no longer with us. Tyke and I would leave Granny's house and walk back to the bus stop at the Navy Yard. We would wait for the W-6 or W8 bus marked for Stanton Road or the Garfield Loop that would take us home. We had fun on those Sunday afternoon bus rides visiting our relatives.

A KICK IN THE BUTT

My friend Leon Robinson and I would take my Daisy Rider B.B. gun and go down to the fence on the boundary line at the rear of our house that separated the house we lived in from the farm properties. Our house was located on the opposite side of the chain link fence in an area between Mr. Evan's and Mr. Mac's farms. Each of the farmers had the following animals on their farm, chickens, turkey, goats, cows, one mule, pigs and two horses. Mr. Mac always had about 50 to 100 little bitty turkeys and chickens running around in the barn yard. Leon and I used to go down to the fence by the chicken barnyard and take target practice using Mr. Mac's chickens and turkey chicks as targets with my B.B. gun. We liked to see them jump up in the air and land on their back with their little feet sticking straight up towards the sky. Leon would always look out for me and me for him, to ensure that no one could sneak up and catch one of us shooting at the chickens. I kept a good look out for Leon when taking his five shots at the chickens; he got two out of five. It was my turn to shoot. Leon gave me the BB gun and I got down on my knees, almost in the prone position, with the B.B. gun barrel sticking through the silver chain link fence. I took a good aim with the gun and got my first bit tie turkey. I cocked the gun and took another aim. That was when I saw stars. Leon spotted Mr. Mac and took off running, and never said a word to me or alerted me that someone was coming. All I could remember was the excruciating pain I felt on my rear end. Mr. Mac had drop-kicked me in the butt with his Sergeant Rock combat boots for killing his chickens. He kicked me so hard in the butt that my whole body was perpendicular with the chain link fence. My butt was hurting so bad I could not talk or say a single word, the tears were flowing from my eyes and snot running out my nose. Mr. Mac grabbed me by the collar of my shirt and dragged me to my house. When my mother saw Mr. Mac dragging me towards our house, she ran outside and asked Mr. Mac to stop and why was he dragging me like that. Mr. Mac said," I caught your son shooting my chickens with his B.B. gun". My mother asked me "Did you shoot Mr. Mac's chickens?", and all I could do was shake my head up and down in the affirmative, yes mama. I would never lie to my mother. She was very upset, and apologized to Mr. Mac for my wrong-doing, and assured him that it wouldn't happen again. Mr. Mac was so mad, that he told my mother that he was going to keep my B.B. gun to cover the cost of all the chickens I had killed in the last couple of months. This was the first time in my life I felt ashamed and sadness. I had embarrassed my mother and my family, and Mr. Mac told my mother that he was going to keep my brand new Daisy Rider B.B. gun for payment of the property I destroyed. I believe that was one of the saddest days in my life as I can remember. I learned a very valuable lesson from that experience. Honor your neighbor as you would want your neighbor to honor you. If you violate this principle, you may spend your valuable time working off the infraction in jail or maybe selling or trading your most valuable possessions to make restitution to the person you dishonored. From the chicken shoot to this day, I have not violated the trust of my neighbors. My definition of a neighbor is anyone with whom I come in contact on a daily basis.

MY FIRST BUSINESS VENTURE

In the summer of 1948, I brought 5 cents' worth of penny candy (two packs of KIXs, two Mary Jane's and one pack of Squirrel Nuts). The KIXs was wrapped taffy four pieces to a pack. Mary Jane's and Squirrel Nuts were packed two individual pieces of candy to a pack. Whenever you had a few pieces of candy, all of your friends would ask for a piece. They would offer you a penny for one individual piece of candy. I sold all the candy and grossed 9 cents profit. I took the money, bought another 14 cents worth of penny candy, and tripled my earnings. The next day, my friend Patsy and I continued to sell candy, and again we doubled our profits. We had $3.00 in profit from the candy sales. Patsy's father Mr. Steward took Patsy and me to the wholesale store and we brought three whole boxes of candy. We no longer split the package of candy, because we could sell the whole pack and make 20 cents profit on each box. We used to go from door to door selling candy to establish our business. Patsy's mother Ms Ann let us use her landing by her front door to sell our candy. Our first month we had made more than $50 in profit. Everybody that lived in the neighborhood knew the location of the candy house. The business was established and we were making money. Soon our net worth was over $300. The saddest thing that happened was when some of the money came up missing, and when I question the looses, Ms Ann accused me of calling her a thief, and told me I could no longer use the landing in her house to sell candy. She gave me $25.00, and told me that I was no longer in the candy business with Patsy. I was hurt and very sad because I was undermined and put out of the business I started. Patsy and I have never lost our friendship because of what had happened to our business. The lessons I learned from that experience is to monitor your business daily, keep your books current, reconcile your receipts and make daily or weekly deposits of your earnings in a bank account. In addition, set up an account with the bank that take at lease two or more signatures to withdraw funds from the business account. My second job, at the age of 10, was as a paper boy for the United Publishing Company, selling The Bulletins. I used to serve fifty establishments, from Sixth Street to Georgetown in the North, to Seventh Street to Twelfth Street to First and O Street in the South-West I was serving bars, pool halls, bowling alleys and restaurants, with The Bulletin contained the daily horse races, numbers and the latest 5 o'clock headline news. I was paid $7.50 a week. When I got my $7.50 paycheck on Friday, I gave my mother $3.50. One dollar was used to purchase a postal savings bond, and 75 cents was used to purchase a book of 10 school bus tickets. I would always spend a dollar to buy something for my mother, such as a dress, a pair of ear-rings or a box of Chinese Egg Foo Young and egg rolls from Coon's Restaurant on 8th and I Street S.E. by the Navy Yard. My money was gone but I had fun and would do it again if I could taste the flavor of the food. Either I was very hungry and the food tasted so good, or it was so good the only way I can get that flavor is to make the food myself. Those were the good old days. I had a newspaper route in Parkland apartments, serving about 200 customers. After serving all of my customers, I had to collect the payment for the weekly service, 30 cents a week and 65% of the people didn't pay. I collected all the newspaper man's money, but my money was always included in the folks who didn't pay for their weekly deliveries, and 20% of my subscribers were three to four weeks behind in their weekly payments. I would collect 100 to $150 for payment to the newspaper route man. My salary for delivering the paper was tired up in uncollected receipts. If I got $2 or $3 I was lucky. I had about approximately $60 tied up in back-payment. You couldn't drop the customers, because they owe you and you had to keep giving them credit or risk losing your investment. The only way to break even was to collect the weekly receipts add what you owed the route man, give him only the money collected and what was owed in back payments. He would get mad when you gave him $25.00 in cash and $80 in credits receipts in the collection book. I quit the news paper route after six months.

THE SOUND OF THE NAVY YARD

My sister and I used to catch the Main Avenue Street Car to visit our Aunt Fanny and Mr. Brown. They had twelve children. Aunt Fanny had diabetes and was legally blind. She had a good heart. I was scared of her for some reason. She was always serious. Consuella and I had so much fun with her younger children Boogie, Grets and Peter. While waiting at the car barn for our bus to depart; I would go to an area on the other side of the street that had many piles of graphite. I would dig in one of the piles of graphite for steel ball-bearings, that we call stealers in the marble game. A little steel marble could break up your opponent's best shooter glass marbles. I believe the piles of graphite were residue from the Naval Gun Factory during that period I do not believe the city was concern with environmental issues. The drilling the large gun barrels for ships at the Gun Factory produced very loud noises on a twenty-four hour basis. The boring of the barrels reminded me of a printing press moving back and forth printing each page of the newspaper. I really didn't know what produce the noise in the gun factory until one day I took my grandchildren for a visit to the Naval Museums at the Navy Yard Gun Factory in the summer of 1987.

THE CABARET

I remember having so much fun at the church cabaret on New Years' Eve. Once or twice a year one of my mother's friends or the Catholic Church would have a cabaret. Everybody would bring their own bottles of whiskey. The church would sell a set up of ice, mixers, and a few glasses that cost from $2 to $5 per table. Each table came with a free bottle of cheap complementary champagne. A ticket to the cabaret entitled you to a chicken or a pork chop dinner to include a dessert. The band would start playing when dinner was over. If you had a ticket to the cabaret, you were somebody. You would let all your friends know that you had a ticket and was going to the cabaret. The cabaret was the time of year you dressed up in your finest clothes. The sequenced dresses and tuxedoes were just starters. The ladies would put on their best make-up and add a little mole just above their lip line. My mother would have her hair perm to be wavy and laid down flat to her head. The women would put on their best rhinestone jewelry and add a little sparkling dust to their face; it sure made them look real pretty under the night-lights. My grandmother would get her best outfit out of mothballs and hang it on the clothes line for about two days to get the mothball smell out of the clothes. When my sister and mother were dressing her, fixing her hair and putting on her make-up, she looked like a sophisticated rich lady. Granny loved to dance and always had a young man hanging on her arm and dancing with her. Now when I look back, most of the men Granny met at the cabaret were of the gay persuasion. When I was growing up, my mother never practiced discrimination. My cousin Peter used to come over to our house and beat all of us in wrestling, and he was on the football team at his high school, and he also took up ballet lessons. We called him by his nickname, Bow. When Bow came out of the closet, his own mother disowned him. I was surprised when I found out. My mother said that she knew it all the time and that was why he could come over to our house and feel comfortable. Many of his friends would come over to our house in drag to play cards and have fun. If you did not know them, you would bet your last dollar you were entertaining some classic women.

A DRUNKEN MIND REVEALS WHAT A SOBER MIND CONCEALS

My dad's name was Charles Roger Hodge Sr. Uncle John called him Saddle low. My grandmother and everybody else called him Roger. My brothers and I called him Charlie Buck. Dad would call himself George Washington, and I don't know the reason why. I remember the year 1979 when Ralph, Aubrey, Charles Wages (my sister's husband) and I came home from the service at the same time. Mom had a big gathering for us, and invited all of the friends we had in the whole neighborhood, because she was so proud to have her sons back home after defending our country. Charlie Buck brought a new Hi-Fi record player on credit. It had a record changer that could play twelve 78-inch records one after another. That night we were all having a good time eating and drinking. Buck was so proud of his boys; he was toasting every 10 or 15 minutes. Buck was feeling no pain at all; that's when we saw Buck come into the living room with his sharp ax and make his statement:" I am George Washington and I'm going to cut down the damn cherry tree." We started to laugh because Buck always had something funny to say. We were waiting in anticipation for the punch line, and it came when Buck drew back the ax and chopped one of the four legs off his new Hi-Fi system, which he hadn't yet paid for. My brothers and I jumped up, grabbed the ax from Buck, and asked him what his problem was. He repeated that he was George Washington. We put him to bed for the night, and the next morning when he woke up from his sleep and saw the leg missing from his Hi-Fi, and found out what he had done, he was sick again. He couldn't believe he did it, until my Mom confirmed that he was portraying George Washington cutting down the cherry tree. Dad was the best dad anyone could have. He always had time for you when he wasn't working. A holiday was the only time Dad had a day off, and he was too tired to play with us. I cannot remember anything bad about my dad. He was a good working family man who first took care of his family. As long as I can remember until his demise, Dad always held down two or three jobs. Dad had only an eighth-grade education. He never talked about his past. Buck was always proud that he had a chance to serve on the Grand Jury in Washington D.C. His picture was on the second page of the Washington Star newspaper. When ever my friends would brag about their dads, I could always say my dad served on the Grand Jury and none of them could match that. They would dispute my claim, challenging me to show the newspaper article, and I did. Charlie Buck was a mild-mannered person who didn't have very much to say unless you said something out of the way to him, or had him in a general conversation. He was well-versed on most subjects, especially politics and American history. Buck would practice silence from Sunday through Thursday. On Friday, Buck and his friends would congregate in the printing room after work at the United Publishing Company, and play a card game called Coon Can. To me, this was like watching a Super Bowl game or a championship soccer match. When Buck came home, he would walk through the house and just say hello when he passed by you, but, on Friday night after he had been drinking gin, he would came home began telling you what you did and did not do on Monday, Tuesday, Wednesday and Thursday. Granny had this saying "a drunken mind reveals what a sober mind conceals". As long as I can remember, I never heard my dad complain about anything, even when the times were rough.

Dad worked hard every day of his life... When dad came home, he gave us a little bit of his time if we didn't have our friends in the house. Otherwise he would eat his dinner and retire for the night.

SUMMERTIME

I remember summertime in Washington D.C. as being the most memorable time for me. School was out for summer vacation. The weather was always hot and muggy. We didn't have air conditioning in those days, and the only way we could cool off was to find a spot under a shade tree or take a walk in the woods. It was always cool there. If you had a penny you could buy a glass of lemonade with a chunk of ice to suck on after finishing the drink. When the heat was unbearable, we would turn on the hose and take a shower. Every once in a while, a firemen from the fire department would turn the water on to check the water pressure in the fire plugs. We could play outside all day long. It was the time of year when, flowers were blooming, the woods were full of blossoms with wild flowers, and the trees were full of green leaves. I remember when I used to walk in the woods and all you could hear was the sound of birds singing and baby birds chirping in their nest. I used to climb up a tree and perch myself on one of the large branches. From that vantage point, I had a clear view of all the wildlife activity on the ground under the tree. On a lucky day, I would see a variety of different animals and birds pass by on the dirt path under the tree. I saw wild rabbits, green garden snakes, stray dogs, rats, cats and many different other species of birds. On a lucky day I could spot a deer, a fox, a muskrat or a beaver. I always liked visiting national parks and the Smithsonian museum. My cousins, Johnny and Marie and I used to go swimming in the pool under Christopher Columbus Fountain at the Union Station. On a good day, the site would be crowded with tourist taking pictures of the monuments. Several tourists would pay one of us for diving off of one of the monuments. Each dive could earn you a dime or a quarter and every once in a while a generous tourist would give you a half dollar for the dive. We did not realize that diving off the monuments into the shallow water was very dangerous because the water was only two and a half to three foot deep. I remember on several occasions I dove off the ledge of one of the monuments and hit my head on the bottom of the pool. I was lucky at that time to come out with only a blooded nose, and another occasion I was knocked unconscious for several minutes and was taken to the hospital. The doctor said I was very lucky that I had not broken my neck. I could have had a spinal cord injury or paralyzed for life. In the summertime, it was always fun to visit the National Parks Services or the District of Columbia Recreation Centers. They were open for Summer Day Camp and would have a full summer program for the underprivileged children. At that time, I did not know I was an underprivileged child. In the 'hood there were three classes of people: the rich, the poor, and the Proctors. If you were very black or very dark with nappy hair, you were considered poor and looked down on no matter what lifestyle or how much money you had. A quote I heard many times was "If you were white or light skinned you were alright, if you were brown you stick around and if you were black you step back". We used to make fun of dark-skinned children who had just come up from the south to live in our neighborhood. We made fun of their tattered clothing and the black high-top boots with little metal loops at the top that they used to wear. We called them jail boots, because we never wore that kind of shoe. We were told that all they ate for breakfast, lunch and dinner were grits and grease, and to always keep a watch out for them because they all were geeches who carried a hook bill knife or a straight razor and would cut your throat if you crossed their path. When we chose sides to play baseball, dodge ball, football and cowboys, we never wanted them on our side. If by chance you had to choose one of them, everybody on the other team would laugh at your team. For some reason, black people in the late 40s and early 50s, was ashamed of their color and wanted to be white. They used to process their hair, and put on skin whitener to bleach their skin. My mother and other ladies were told that they could get rid of their flat noses by sleeping with a clothes pin clipped on their nose. Summertime was the time to go fishing in the Potomac River, or as we called it, the Anacostia River. I remember when I caught a 4 or 5-pound carp, and took it home to my grandmother and she stuffed it and baked it. That was the best fish I can remember eating. In the springtime, we would go down to the mall by the Lincoln Memorial to see the cherry blossom blooms on the cherry trees that Japan gave to the United States that were lined along side of the reflection pool. We would also line up on Constitution Avenue for the Cherry Blossom Parade. The summertime in Washington D.C. was the prettiest time of the year for me. The new fruits pushed the pink and white blossoms off the trees. The first fruit tree to bear fruit was the cherry tree. We knew the location of most of the fruit trees in our neighborhood. We would risk our lives to climb into somebody's yard to get a few cherries. The caretaker would shoot at us with a blast from a shotgun or rifle. I remember on this one particular day Mr. Mac, the caretaker at the Jewish Graveyard on 15th Place South East Washington D.C. caught us stealing pare from a pear tree on the synagogue's grounds. Mr. Mac said that he was shooting his shotgun over the children's heads to scare them and several of the stray pellets from the shot gun hit and killed one of my friends who was climbing back over the graveyard fence after taking some of the pears off one of the trees behind the Jewish Synagogue. A young boy's life was lost and Mr. Mac's life was ruined for a couple of pears. Every other Saturday or Sunday, dad would take the entire family and any of our friends for a ride in the company's truck. We would pile in the back of his truck for a ride into the country. Dad would sometime take us to the beaches or to several juke joints or night clubs in Waldolf, Upper Marlboro or Saint Mary's County Maryland. Mom would fry up a couple of chickens to include a couple packages of chicken backs, necks, and livers, Mom would also fry up about 10 to 12 pork chops and make them into sandwiches to carry on the trip. She would also make a large bowl of potato salad and a large pan of string beans. On our way to the beach, dad would stop at one of the fruit and vegetable stands at a turn-off on the highway to buy a large North Carolina watermelon. Watermelons grown in North Carolina were large with an oblong shape with green and white stripes running along the length of the melon. North Carolina watermelons in those days were large and fat with a 20- to 30-inch girth, and weighing in from 20 to 30 pounds. The melons at the roadside stands were stored in a large brown wooden barrel about four and a half foot in height and three feet in circumference. There were three large metal bands wrapped around barrels to hold it together. The barrels were filled with watermelons and covered with chunks of slivered ice to keep the melons cool. My dad was an expert when it came to selecting a sweet ripe watermelon. Dad had a special technique he used to select the ripest, sweetest melon. He taught me how to thump a watermelon by plucking it with my index finger and listen for the hollow sound. He also showed me where to look for a dark brown spot he called the sugar spot at the end opposite the stem end of the melon. The bigger the brown spot the sweeter the melon. Dad was a master at picking the sweetest watermelon from the barrels. Once we got into Waldolf Maryland, Pat & G-G's restaurant was our first stop. It was a gray square one-storey building with light gray edging and the name written in silver 'Pat & G G's'on the large sign on top of the building. They had a big barbecue pit in front of the parking lot. We never had enough money to buy anything from the barbecue pit. The aroma from the beef and pork ribs and whole pigs cooking over hot glowing red and white hot coals with the smell of the hickory wood smoke and the aroma from the cooked meat. In my mind, I can only imagine how good that barbecue must have tasted. When approaching the entranceway to Pat & G-G's, the smell of stale beer coming from the exhaust fan mounted in a window next to the front entrance door saturated the entire area around the building... Upon entering the building, the first thing you saw was three rows of slot machines in the center of the floor. On the right side of the restaurant was an open stand-up bar. The left side was set up for dining with several badly worn out Japanese chrome-trimmed gray tables and several unsafe chairs with bent or broken legs. On The back wall next to the rest rooms were two large mirrors shaped like a wavy sliding board. When you stood in front of the mirrors, one would show you as being fat and the other one would show you being skinny and distorted. The juke box had all the latest blues and rock and roll 45 records and was located in the rear corner of the building. For one dollar you could play any five of your favorite records. The wooden floor was covered with sawdust to absorb the sweat from the dancers and keep the floor dry. The juke box played continuously, and there was always one or two couples dancing throughout the building. I will never forget the sounds of the coins being dropped into the slot machines, and the noise from the lever on the one-arm bandit being pulled to start the wheels rotating. If you were a winner, you heard the sweet sound of bells and pulsating sirens while the coins were dropping on to the hollow metal tray at the bottom of the slot machines. The sound of the music from the juke box and people talking loud and laughing with joy was a happy moment in time. All of the children were running around and having fun dancing, playing tag and sliding in the sawdust; I remember the sounds of the bartender popping open and sitting the beer bottles on the bar. These were some of the sounds and fun I had at Pat & G-G's and the other juke joints in Maryland. The Moon Light Inn and Blue Bird Inn were no more then 50 to 100 yards down the dirt road. When the sun went down, everybody would congregate at the Moon Light Inn for dancing to the music of a live band. At the Moonlight Inn, buying a bushel of crabs included your entrance fee for dancing; otherwise you would have to pay a one dollar cover charge to enter the dance hall and the listen to the rhythm and blues band singing and playing their songs. I would dance to just about every song that the live band played or music played on the juke box during the live band's intermissions , Because it was so hot and muggy, the sweat from most of the dancers would be dripping on the floor and would cause an unsafe condition. For safety reasons, the owners put sawdust on their floors to prevent a dancer from slipping and injuring themselves. The Moon Light Inn cooked some of the best-tasting steamed crabs on the East Coast. My dad would always buy two bushels of crabs. To keep the flies out, the crab eating area was surrounded with screens located in the picnic area. The crab eating area had six large wooden tables with 10 folding wooden chairs. The tables were lined with newspapers, and condiments of hot sauce, vinegar and paper napkins and a crab cracker. They would serve the red hot cooked male and female Chesapeake Bay Crab by the bushel baskets with hot white steam still rising from the basket as they were delivered to your table. The waiter would empty the bushel basket of hot crab out onto the newspaper on the long picnic table, and the family crab feast would begin. We were given a minimum of three crabs each. It helped if you knew how to identify the devil fingers, and to clean and discard them from the crab's body. I believe I could have eaten at least ten. They tasted so good. I learned to pick and clean the meat from crabs at an early age. We had many superstitious beliefs in our culture. We were told not to eat crabs if you had first eaten ice cream or watermelon, because it would give you a bad stomachache and could kill you. They would always tell a story about someone who died after eating ice cream and crabs. Some of the other superstitions were if someone sweeps you with a broom you had to spit on it or you were going to jail soon. If you broke a mirror it was seven years bad luck. You could reverse your luck if you tossed a handful of salt over your left shoulder. If you had a dream about fish, someone close to you was pregnant. One that I always used with my children was when a baby tried to stand up and showed signs of wanting to walk; I would stand the baby in a corner of a room and brush the baby's legs seven times with a broom, and let the child come out of the corner by it self. Every child that I have performed this superstitious practice on began to walk in two weeks. I have had 100% success rate on this superstitious practice.

NEIGHBORHOOD LEGENDS

The Fredrick Douglass projects dwellings produced several legends. Billy Stewart was a renowned blues musician. We used to call him Ooodie Bear because he was so fat. He had several top blues hit records during the 50s and 60s. He was rather large in stature, and he looked like the Pillsbury Dough boy. The only difference was the Pillsbury Dough boy was white, and Ooodee Bear was black. I remember the times when my mother invited Ooodee Bear into our house and he would sing the blues and the latest rock and roll songs to entertain the crowd. People came to our house to participate in my mother's rent party. He would sing his love songs and the people would give him tips. He was a funny guy, always joking and getting himself in trouble. I remember on one occasion he took one of the maintenance department's three-wheeled scooters and started it up and began to drive it around and around in circles. He was stuck on the scooter and couldn't get off because he didn't know how to cut it off. He was yelling, screaming and crying at the same time. He was so funny that we laughed and cried until our stomachs ached. .Ooodee Bear got in big trouble and his mother had to go to the office to pay for the property damage he cause while riding that scooter. Ooodie Bear won a lot of local and regional singing talents contest, and he went on to became one of the great recording blues and jazz artist under his original name Billy Stewart. John Thomas who lived in our neighborhood was one of the greatest basketball players and coaches of all time; he lived across the street from my house on Fredrick Place with his mother and two sisters. I remember John and I used to shoot marbles on our knees in the dirt in his back yard. John was a well-mannered young man who always treated everybody with respect. John never used his size to resolve a problem when we were growing up. I can truly say he was never a bully. John was a person who liked to have fun and play sports, mainly basketball. We used to play basketball with a tennis ball late in the evening, by the light of the moon on the basket ball courts at Turner Elementary School. We both attended Our Lady of Perpetual Help Catholic Church. We used to spend a lot of quality time together. Jimmy Harps was another friend of mine growing up in the 'hood. He became a renowned jazz piano player. He was also a great saxophone player and played with several renowned blues and jazz artist and their bands. I remember on many occasions I would visit Jimmy's house, located on top of the hill on Fredrick Place. He and his mother use to live alone in a small two bedroom single-storey bungalow house. Jimmie was his mother's only child. Jimmy was not spoiled and would always share his talents and anything he owned with you. He was always a very pleasant person to be associated with. I believe Jimmy Harps and Billy Stewart's families were the only two houses that had pianos in our neighborhood. Our neighborhood had three sports legends that lived across the street from my house. Ralph Boston was an Olympic medal-winning runner, and Ronald Tyner an Olympic sprinter and high jumper and John Thompson a Basketball player for the Boston Celtics. Junior Tyler was a young adult gangster who lived on Stanton Terrace with his mother, father and seven brothers and sisters. He was very popular in the 'hood until he made a mistake of robbing and killing two guards at the Laingsburg department store. He was charged and convicted of first-degree murder and was sentence to death in the electric chair.. Junior Tyler was the last person to be executed in the electric chair in the Washington D.C. City Jail.

JONING:

Joning was considered a status symbol in the 'hood. Life in the hood and living in the projects was hard as hell if your family was labeled poor. The grownups and children in the 'hood used the following criteria for labeling a poor family: If your family didn't have enough food to last until Friday and you had to borrow food from one of your neighbors, your house was nasty, dirty and full of roaches, you didn't have shades in your windows, but instead you had dirty white sheets hanging in the windows, your skin was ashy (needed lotion) and you smelled like urine (or pee, as we used to say)

because either you or your sister or brother urinated on you while sleeping in the bed, you had holes in your socks and shoes and your feet stank, you always wore hand-me-down clothes, you ate grits and fatback for breakfast, beans with salt pork or fried potato and onion for dinner, your bag lunch had syrup sandwiches made with homemade biscuits, you did not have a bicycle or wagon to ride and your little sister or brother had a snotty nose. It was very hard, or as we would say, it was tough living in the projects, especially if your peers or so-called friends labeled your family as being poor. You really caught hell, especially if you were the butt of a joning (joke) session. The joning were rhymes used by one person to insult the other person's mother or family member. The rhymes were sexual and vulgar in nature. Joning were rhymes with sayings that would make everybody laugh hysterically at what was said about you or your family. To start a jone, the first person would take the lead of talking about the other person's mother or living situation. You had the know how to start the joning and how to respond to a good jone. For example, "I hate to talk about your mother, she's a clean old soul, she has a tin can pussy and a rubber asshole, she got hairs on her snatch to sweep the floor, she has keys on her ass that locked the door, damn that lady for Baltimore, any more from Chicago". The other person who the jone was directed at would give a response like this: "I f@$k your mother on top of the hill, can't anybody get her but me and Bob Steal." The other person would respond with "I did it to your mother on top of a fence, the fence split, she shit, I didn't get nothing but a little bit. I jammed your mother on top of a heater she got off and burnt my peter. I jammed your mama on top of the house, can't nobody get her but me and Mickey Mouse. Joning on each-other could go on for hours, or until one person ran out of jones or started to cry. I have seen some of my peers get so enraged and angry with hate from the joning that I believed that person could, and sometimes they would, do harm to the person who was joning on them. I used to stand around and listen to the joner and try to remember all their jones, because I knew that my day would come and I would need the words and sayings to defend my family and myself. I remember almost all of the jones I heard, and I was one of the best joners in the 'hood. No body wanted to get in a joning contest with me because I had more than enough sayings, and I could go on for hours and wouldn't stop until I made the other person look or feel bad, and sometimes cry. The word got out in the 'hood "Don't jone with Junior Hodge, because he is one of the best joners around." I was bad; I never lost a joning contest. However, if the person I was joning against got mad, and if he was bigger than me, he would resort to violence and beat me up. Joning to me was a sense of relief, and to be labeled one of the best joners in our neighborhood gave me pride. To me, it was something to be proud of during that period of my life. Looking back to that time of my life, I believe that joning on someone's mother or family was cruel and unusual punishment, and knowing how I feel today, I apologize to anyone I hurt by joning on them or their family. If you were the winner in the joning contest, everybody would join in with you laughing, and would continue taunting the loser about the jones. It seemed as though everybody who was in the audience when the joning took place would always take sides with the winner. We had some of the meanest children in our neighborhood and they would continue to agitate the loser until he would get so mad that he would try to fight the entire group of 5 to 10 children who were taunting him. Only the winner would survive the humiliation. The talk about the joning contest would go on for several weeks or until someone else was joned down. You had to be very careful when you were joning on another person's mother. First of all you better be a good fighter or the person to whom you were joning on could beat you up. You had to be careful who you challenge or had to defend your honor because If the person who you were joning on was bigger than you and you out-joned him, he had but one course of action to protect his honor and that was to take out his vengeance on you with his fist. If the person you were joning lost the joning session, he would try to beat you up in a fight. Even though you won the joning contest, you were not considered the winner of the joning session if you lost the fight. To this day I can not figure out why I was always a target of the bullies in my neighborhood. My father told me to fight, even if the odds were against me. The day I began to fight back with words, and use what ever I could get my hands on to physically fight and hurt the bullies who tried to inflict bodily harm on me , the days of bulling little Junior Hodge were over.

SWEET POTATO PIES

Mr. and Ms Goodman who were senior citizens living in our neighborhood. Mr. Goodman loss his leg in world war. I and had a wooden peg leg strapped to his upper thigh. Mr. Goodman use to push a wheelbarrow up and down the street looking for junk to sell to the junkyard. Mrs. Goodman was blind and ran a bakery shop out of her pantry. She sold fresh baked small individual sweet potato pies out of her back door. All of the kids who lived on Stanton Terrace knew that she was blind, and every once in a while we would take advantage of her handicap. Even though Ms Goodman was blind, she always kept a clean well-organized house. She knew where everything was located in her house. She stored her individual pies for sale on several wooden shelves that were made by Mr. Goodman and located in the pantry area by the kitchen door. We would ring her front door bell and when Mrs. Goodman came to the front door to take our order for pies and she would tell you to meet her at the kitchen door to pick up your purchase. At the same time some of the boys in the neighborhood devised a scheme to trick her, by ringing her door bell for her to come to the front door, then they would sneak in the back door and steal a few of her pies. The families in our neighborhoods were a close-knit group who stuck together through thick and thin. If you did something bad in the 'hood it was like front page news. Everybody in the neighborhood knew the details by 4 o'clock that evening. The 'hood was like the neighborhood watch program of today. Everybody looked out for everybody else. When we stole the pies from Ms Goodman's pantry, it was a known fact that our parents would find out what we had done and we would have to do some type of community work to pay back the Goodman's for the pieces of candies and baby sweet potato pies we stole out of their storage pantry. This was a lesson I learned early in my life, that you must always work hard to secure the things you desire and reframe from stealing thing that someone else have worked hard for.

DOUGLASS JUNIOR HIGH SCHOOL

The environment at Douglass Junior High school was no better than the environment at Anita Turner Elementary School. It was the continuing saga of "Let's pick on little Junior Hodge." Through all the adversities, I managed to fall in love with a girl for the first time in my life. Vivian Robinson was my first puppy love. She was so kind to me and looked past my poverty, and she treated me equally with all other people. Eventually Vivian and I fell in love. Vivian gave me hope, even though her parents were not too fond of me. I believe that Vivian's parent's felt sorry for me because and treated me unfairly because I didn't have the best of clothes and they assume that I was trash and not good for their daughter future because my family was poor and I did not have anything to offer Vivian. The black people who lived in the projects had their own discrimination practices. I felt more discriminated in my own culture or neighborhood among blacks then I did among the white segregationist whom my parents shield us from. Discrimination in the black neighborhood was determined by your features, your hair texture the shade of your skin, and material things (toys, bicycles, and if your family had an automobile). For the two years Vivian and I were girlfriend and boyfriend, her parents never invited me over or allowed me into their home. To this day, I still do not understand why they had such a dislike for me. I was always respectful in every way. I would always walk to and from school with Vivian carrying her books. In those days a boy carrying girls books showed shivery and it was an indication to everybody that she was your girlfriend. Every once in a while I would see Vivian looking out of one of her windows on my way home from the local grocery store. She would call me to come over to her bedroom window when she saw me passing by her house. I used to stand outside of her window in the cold and inclement weather for hours talking to her. I was always taught by my mother to be respectful to women and above all things not to hurt them physically or mentally. I whole heartily respected Vivian and never violated her trust. The only thing we did as girlfriend and boyfriend we would passionately kiss each-other. Her kisses would always send cold chills up and down my spine. Just the thought of her kisses would make me feel good. At that time in my life, I really didn't have sex or anything else on my mind, maybe because I didn't know anything about sex and why my body felt so strange when I kissed a girl. It never felt that way when I kissed my mom or grandmother. Because I was not educated on the facts of life in my adolescence years, today I know the reason why I had those strange feeling that came over my entire body whenever I passionately kissed Vivian. Vivian use to get mad with me because I did not touch her sexually during some of our passionate moments. When I look back to those times, I believe a dead cat was on the line in the sexual arena of our love life and giving me a lot of help I did not need. Our relationship was resolved when she became pregnant at the age of 14. I wasn't really hurt, because I was not educated on how a woman got pregnant or what pregnancy was all about. Smoking in the boys' restroom I remember when we used to smoke cigarettes in the boys' restroom. After each class we had ten minutes to report to our next classroom. If you had a cigarette, this was the time to have a smoke break. The bullies would always be there to take your cigarettes from you. I used to go into one of the toilet stalls to light mine, and as soon as they saw the smoke, they would bang on the stall door a demand a drag from your cigarette. They would take it and never return it to you. If you asked for it back, they would kick you in the butt or slap you in the face. The bullies were mean and it seemed as though I was always a target for their enjoyment. We would smoke until one of the school monitors, a teacher or the principal broke into the restroom. If you were caught smoking, you were given a five-day suspension from school and 12 licks on your rear end by Fanny Dorsey, our principal, who seemed to get pleasure using a wooden paddle with holes drilled in it. The holes were drilled in the paddle to eliminate the air between the paddle and you felt the full impact the paddle when it hit your butt.

WHERE DO BABIES COME FROM?

I was sheltered and didn't learn about the facts of life until I was 21 years old. I believed and never doubted anything my mother told me. When my mother was pregnant and it was time for her to have her baby, instead of telling me she was going to the hospital, she told me that she was going to the Murphy's 5 &10 variety store to get us a new baby, and I truly believed every word that proceeded from my mother's mouth. I didn't know anything about the life-cycles. The only thing I knew was that God made me to love him and serve him and to be happy with him in heaven. I started working when I was nine years old. I became a victim of integration. The white teachers put up with us because we were integrated in a white school. Many of black students who attended the integrated schools did not have the opportunity to select courses leading to a college education. We were given general academic courses in woodworking, sewing, sheet metal, cooking and the basic electives (English, math and history). We were told that the other classes were full. Blacks were never given the opportunity to take classes such as typing, printing, journalism or advance math subjects that would have prepared us for a college education. The school counselor did not motivate us to pursue academic subjects for continuous education.

HIGH SCHOOL

I remember distinctly the first day my black school friend and I tried to integrate at Anacostia High School, on September 3, 1956. It was one of the saddest days in my life. On my way to school, I had to pass through several white neighborhoods. From the time my friends and I reached the white neighborhood, we were called all kinds of names. "Go home niggers, we don't want no coons in our school, niggers don't belong in white schools, you don't belong here, go back to Africa where you came from, look at the monkeys trying to come to our school, go back to your cages in the Washington Zoo, you are in the wrong neighborhood you little baboons!" I really couldn't comprehend what was going on. This was the first time I felt what my black brothers and sisters was going through and feeling in the southern states. I was terrorized, scared, and sick to my stomach, especially when we arrived at Anacostia High School the next day escorted by the U.S. Marshals and numerous white students and their parents stood in front of the entrance doors of the school to block us and denying us entry into the school. Segregation was at its peak in 1956. My parents were good at keeping segregation and poverty away from us. We used to read about all the injustice that was done to our people in the Southern States, and never knew we had the same segregation practices in Washington D.C. As I look back over my life, I can remember the times my friends and I went to Fairlawn Public Park and tried to get into the public swimming pool, and was turned away. They told us the pool was full. I remember when we used to go to the Little Tavern Hamburger Shoppe to get a ten cent hamburger; we had to go to the side of the building to order one. I thought the window on the side of the building was where you could get a fast order to go. I wasn't aware that blacks could not sit down at a counter in a restaurant to eat or order something and the People's Drug Store was no better. I remember on this one day I sit on one of the stools in the People's Drug store for an hour without being ask if I needed service when an old black gentlemen came up to me and said "Son, if you want to order something, you have to go to the end of the counter." I also encountered segregation when we used to take a Sunday ride on the street car to the end of the line at 17 Street and Burney Circle S.E. There was a hotdog stand in the circle, and all the white people could go inside and sit down to make their order. Blacks could not go into the facility; they had to order from the side window. I always wondered why I couldn't go to the big amusement park in Glen Echo Maryland. When I was growing up, I always thought that Washington D. C. was in the north; until I visited my sister in-law Pat and her husband Ellis and saw a large sign stretched across the highway stating that you were crossing the Mason Dixon Line from Maryland state line into Pennsylvania. For many years I used to get angry and verbally attack someone if they said that Washington D.C. was in the south. Several of my northern friends would make fun and say the letters D C stood for deep in the country.' I have to attest that the saying was true. The only place I remember going where I didn't feel or experience segregation was at the Washington Zoo. I believe segregation was present all over town but our parents protected us from it by only taking us to establishments that catered to blacks. I used to base discrimination on riding the buses or street cars. In Washington D.C. we could sit anywhere on public transportation so I thought we were among the northern states. I can't remember experiencing discrimination in Atlantic City or New Jersey. Back in the 1950s and 60s, the Jet and Ebony always had articles in their magazines depicting how our black brothers and sisters were falsely accused and arrested, shot, bitten by dogs, or killed by lynching just because they were trying to exercise there constitutional rights. If they tried to sit in a seat at the front of the bus they would be put in jail or murdered if the put up a fight or said the wrong word or talked back to a white person. I thought that since we lived in Washington D.C. and had a choice to whether or not we wanted to sit in the front or the back of the bus, I thought D.C was among the northern state. I did not find out until later in my adult life that Washington D.C. was a southern district located in the south.

THE CHRISTMAS HOLIDAYS

Christmas time of year was a special moment in my life. It was that time of year that everybody seemed to be happy and anticipating that great day the birth of our Lord and savior Jesus Christ. All of the lamp-posts and pine trees on the streets all over town and in our neighbor hood were decorated with garland, Christmas lights, ornaments and candy canes. My father would always take me with him into the woods to select our Christmas tree. Dad and I would walk through out the woods looking for the best tree among the hundreds at many different size trees. Dad would always select the prettiest fullest Christmas tree in the woods. He would pick a tree that was between 14 to 16-feet tall that had a year's growth on the top. Dad would use his sharp ax to cut down the tall tree. After downing the tree, he would cut off the top of the tree and take it home to be decorated. Dad said that the top of a tall tree was the best part of the tree and it would last throughout the holiday season, because the sap was captured in the top, and the tree would not dry out like most other trees. Dad and I would drag the tree out of the woods to the side of the road, where we would load it on to my Red Rider wagon to transport it home. On our way home we had to pass by several of our neighbor's houses and when they saw us coming they would come out of their house and ask my dad where did he get such a beautiful Christmas tree. Dad always kept it a secret and would not tell anybody the location or where we got our Christmas tree from. Dad response was "We got this tree off of a Christmas tree farm in Maryland." Once we got the tree home, I had to make a wooden stand for our Christmas tree. All year long I would save empty cantaloupe boxes that I got out of the dumpster behind Dave's Supermarket on Alabama Avenue. Besides making Christmas tree stands I also made children little lawn chairs out of those wooden cantaloupe boxes. After making the wooden stand and attaching it to the Christmas tree, we would stand it up for display in the selected corner of the living room, and my job was done. My mother and my sister Consuella would get out the Christmas tree decorations and ornaments from last year and start decorating the Christmas tree. Throughout the year, Mom would always collect some of the most unique trinkets and ornaments she could find or buy from the goodwill or thrift stores. In my mind eye, I always thought that after the tree was decorated, the stage was set for the birth of Christ and in preparation for Santa Claus to visit our house and bring us lots of toys, candies, fruit and nuts for our Christmas stockings we hung on the wall on Christmas Eve. Once the tree was decorated and the lights were turned on, we had done our part and we could do nothing else but be patient and wait for that glorious day to come. I used to hear my parents and other adults say "Christmas is just around the corner". I was always curious to know where that corner was. I was always looking around to corners of buildings trying to find Christmas. The temperature in Washington in December was generally cold during the Christmas time of year. We were always looking for snow during the Christmas Season, and most of the time we was blessed with a good snow fall. I used to think that if it did not snow Santa Claus would not be able come to our house because he did not have wheels on his sleigh. Santa Clause always made it to the houses in my neighborhood, even if we didn't have snow for that year. The air seem to have had a special fragrance, the smell of pine trees, burning wood and the smell and the aroma of baking bread, cookies, pies and cakes throughout our neighborhood. The week before Christmas, Carolers from all over town would go from house to house throughout our housing development singing Religious songs and Christmas Carols. They would always end up singing my favorite Christmas songs, Jingle Bells, Frosty the Snow Man and Rudolf the Red-Nosed Reindeer. We would go down to the mall to see the national Christmas tree in front of the White House. All of the department store's windows were filled with Christmas displays and the new toys that were available that year. The Hecht's Company used to have moving Christmas displays in all of their display windows, The moving displays were scenes with Santa's elves building toys, Ms Claus cooking for Santa Clause, happy children building a snow man, ice skating, throwing snowballs, playing in the white snow, Santa Claus on the roof top going down a chimney, children riding on their sleighs, horses pulling a sleighs and Santa Clause with a sleigh full of toys being pulled by his reindeers. The scene was set and the Christmas music was being played from the loud speakers outside of almost every store in the downtown shopping district. Everybody shopping in the area could hear the music playing as they were walking up and down the street looking at the Christmas displays in the windows. There were street vendors lined along the curb on every block and on every corner of the street selling hot sweet potatoes, and roasted bags of chestnuts. It seemed as though the smell of apples and oranges sold by the vendors was in the air all around the shopping environment. Those smells during the Christmas are etched in my mind and are still in my senses after 60 years. Back in those days I believe you had to personally go to see Santa Clause and set down on his knee and tell him personally what you wanted him to bring me for Christmas. It was a must in my mind; otherwise Santa would not leave me anything under the Christmas tree on Christmas day. The days leading up to Christmas were not always full of fun, and we still had chores to do. The chore I hated the most, and it seemed to always come during the Christmas season, was shoveling a ton of coal off the street where the coal man had dropped it from his truck. I had to transport the ton of coal from the street to the coal bin on our front porch with a little 2- to 3-gallon black tin coal bucket. It was very hard and tiresome to carry the coal from the pile on the street to the coal bin on the step by our front door. It could take from 4 to 5 hours to move that ton of coal using my small bucket. The time could be cut in half if you could get one or two of your friends to help you move the coal. However, when your friends saw the coal being dropped on the street, they seem to disappear and were nowhere to be found until after the coal was put into the coal bin. We also had to chop the wood used for lighting the coal in the stove. I had to set up the wood stove that heated the house. I would first shake the stove to remove all the ashes from the grates, and then clean all the ashes out of the bottom of the stove. I would then twist up a lot of newspaper and lay it on the grate, add a little wood to cover the paper and then add a shovel or two of coal on top of the wood. You would then set the flue to half way, to get a good draft. You could now open the bottom of the stove and light the newspaper and hope that the wood started to burn and the coal would light, otherwise you would have to start all over again. After the coal started to burn, you could add more coal to the fire and set the flue to three-quarters closed to slow down the burning. You would also crank the stove with the stove crank to remove some of the small ashes. During the Christmas season we would make a split in the water chestnuts and put them in a pan or in the hot ashes that fell from the steel grate at the bottom of the stove, and cook them. They were the best tasting chestnuts I have ever eaten. Christmas was the best time of year to sell wood to our neighbors. It was a good time of year for paperboys also, because most of the subscribers would give you a Christmas tip in appreciation for delivering their newspapers throughout the year. Most of the customers I served and to include the nasty and disgruntled ones would have the spirit of love in their heart during the Christmas season. I would sometimes look up into the sky hoping that I might by chance get lucky and see Santa Claus's sleigh with his reindeers streaking across the sky with a sleigh full of toys. I would always volunteer to help clean the house, the front yard and anything else my mom wanted me to do. I used to lie down in my bed and daydream about the things I asked Santa Claus to bring me. I was so sure that Santa Claus would honor my wishes. I was grateful for what was left under the tree for me, even though none of the toys that I asked for were there. I wanted a set of Tom Mix guns with a holster, and all I got was a plastic click gun that did not pop caps. It just went click when you pulled the plastic trigger' and click when you let the trigger go back to its original position. All of my friends would make fun of my little plastic guns. I asked Santa for a bicycle and got a little red wagon and a pair of hot buster skate that would not stay clamped to your shoes. If you were skating down the hill on your skates one or two times, you would wear a hole in the metal wheels. Everything I got for Christmas was so cheap that the toys would ware out or be broken in one or two days. I did not abuse my toys, even though they were cheap. I always accepted what was given to me. My parents gave me the best they could afford, and they made me feel rich even though, monetarily, we were considered poor. I was always proud of what ever was given to me, and never looked at the quality. I always thought of the goodness in the person's heart who gave me the gift. My father and mother gave me the most precious gift anyone could receive, and that was the gift of love and understanding. They taught me not to be hung up on material things, and to make good with what you have. I have always used that philosophy, and have been successful with it. On Christmas morning, we would get up at 5 o clock in the morning just before the sun began to rise and tried to be the first one downstairs to open up our presents. The first thing I wanted to see was what Santa had put in the old socks that my dad used to wear. On Christmas Eve we would hang the old socks on one of the nails we put on the wall for Santa to fill with goodies. On Christmas day our socks were filled with the same items that were put in the socks on the previous year. The socks were filled Christmas candy, peppermint candy canes, and some other loose candy stuck together with one apple and one orange and a couple of pencils. I cannot remember if anything else was put in the socks. Mom and Granny would start cooking breakfast and Christmas dinner early in the morning. Breakfast on Christmas day was fried chicken smothered with onions, green peppers and pan gravy served with country grits, eggs, fried potatoes, biscuits and hot cocoa or coffee. For dinner we had home-made rolls, a large tom turkey stuffed with oyster dressing, macaroni and cheese, collard greens, corn pudding, cabbage cooked with fat back or strick of lean, string beans, bake beans and candied yams on the side. For dessert, we had several sweet potato, egg custard and apple pies, yellow pound cake, rice pudding and my favorite, bread pudding with raisins and nuts. We would sometimes have a fruitcake and a mincemeat pie. When dad and mom had a good year, they would send me to Stefan's bakery to get a coconut cake and a peach pie. Steffon's Bakery was one of the best bakeries in the District of Columbia Metropolitan area. People would come from miles around and stand in line for two or three hours waiting to buy a hot just out of the oven fresh baked coconut pound cake, rum cake or a peach cherry or French apple pie.

MILITARY SERVICE

At the age of 19, I joined the United States Air Force on September 10, 1959. I was motivated to join the Air Force because my sister Consuella's husband Bruce Woodland and her common-law husband Rocky Pool they were both in the Air Force. I was crazy about the blue Air Force uniform. In addition, I needed a break away from the life cycle of living in the projects. I decided to make a career out of the Air Force and served honorably from September 9, 1959 to March 31, 1983. I retired after 23 years and 6 month at Bolling Air Force Base and was given the Meritorious Service Medal. The Air Force recruiter promised and offered us a lot to join the military service and delivered little or nothing, The recruiter told me if I join the Air Force and made it my career, I would never have to pay for any medical or dental care for the rest of my life and that was one of the biggest lies ever told by the recruiters. Today we have been stripped of our promise dental care, and now as retiree I have to purchase Tri Care Insurance to receive any medical care at a base hospital. The commissary is the only major benefit I still have and that seem to be in an unstable status. After making up my mine to join the military, I took and passed the military entrance examination at the Air Force Recruiting office on Twelfth and F Street, North West Washington D.C. After passing the military entrance test and I was inducted and sworn into the Air Force at an army base in Baltimore, Maryland. I received all of my military shots and was given a military service number 13668135. Over the years, our social security number took the place of our military service number. All of the new inductees were put on a C-54 airplane and was flown to Lackland Air Force Base in San Antonio Texas. I was assigned to basic training flight 685 where I began my 8 weeks of basic military training. Being away from home for the first time and living in an unfamiliar surroundings made basic training very hard and stressful. I had a problem eating, sleeping and taking a shower with groups of people of who were of different races and back grounds. There was no privacy and I was not used to undressing or taking a shower in front of other people nor could I get used to using an open toilet. Because of the new environment I was forced to live in during my basic training it allowed me to quickly adapt and overcome the fear I had of being naked in front of other people. Our flight had members from all walks of life. We had country boys and city slickers, and airman who were of different nationalities and religions. We also had several die-hard segregationists who practice racism and hatred. They had numerous problems trying to adapt or adjust to living with people of different race and religious backgrounds. Some of them were able to adjust and the ones who couldn't were given a general discharge for unfit for military service under honorable condition. Technical Sergeant Tucker was the name of my basic training instructor. He had red hair and his skin was reddish color with numerous freckles on his face. Sgt Tucker was a tough Training Instructor (TI). My first encounter with TSgt Tucker was a knee boot in the butt for laughing in ranks when we first arrived at Lackland Air Force Base. After kicking me in the butt, Sgt Tucker gave me the job as the flight's chow runner. A chow runner was a designated representative appointed by the Training Instructor to run to the dining facility (Chow Hall) and request permission from the Mess Checker to bring our flight over on the sidewalk leading to the front entrance to the chow hall. I had to count all the members of my flight as they went through the entrance door to the Chow Hall. The chow runner was the last one in my flight to go through the chow line and to eat. I had to eat in a hurry because my flight could not leave the chow hall until I had finish eating. The first week of my basic military training was the hardest, because this was my first time being away from home by myself. I missed my family and friends, and it seemed as though I had lost my freedom. After a few weeks of basic training most of the members in my flight became friends and supported each-other. I experienced good camaraderie with most of the members in my flight. On a normal day we had to get out of the bed at the sound of reveille at 4 am in the morning. You had only 20 minute to make your bed ready for inspection, hurry and take a shower, put, on your clothes and boots and line up outside in a military formation and be ready for inspection. After the inspection our flight instructor would march us to the parade ground to do our morning basic training exercises. I was not a physical fit person and could do no more than three chin-ups or four push-ups at the most. Eventually I was able to pass the entire fitness test. My favorite part of basic training was going on the night patrol marches and running through the woods. I hated going through the gas chamber because it took away my breath, burned my eyes and it was hard for me to breathe. To me, that was the toughest challenges of my basic training. My family and friends were happy that I had chosen to join the military service, as it was my way to get out of the ghetto and pursue a military career. The military service gave me a chance to travel and meet new friends. I entered the Air Force with the rank of Airman basic and over the years I was promoted to Master Sergeant and honorably retired after in 23 years and 6 months of military service. I was trained in three different career fields. I worked as an Electrical Power Production Technician when I was stationed overseas. That job consisted of operating the power generating plants that provided electrical power to the installations. I also preformed periodic inspection, overhauled and repaired generator sets and associated equipment to include diesel and gasoline engines and water pumps. When I was stationed in the Continental United States, I worked as an Aerospace Ground Equipment Repairman. I worked on all associated equipment for testing and starting military fighter and jet bomber aircraft. My first assignment after basic training was to Sheppard Air Force base, in Wichita Falls, Texas to attend the technical training school for Power Production Technicians. After graduating from the training school I was assigned to Elmendorf Air Force base in Anchorage, Alaska. I was assigned to the 334 Engineering Squadron Power Production Shop. I was a member of a roaming maintenance team that travel to remote sites throughout Alaska performing periodic inspections and repair on diesel and gasoline engines, water pumps and generator sets. I also operated a power generating plant at the Nak Nak Lake military fishing camp in King Salmon, Alaska. Upon completion of my service in Alaska, I was assigned to the 556th Strategic Missile Squadron at Plattsburgh Air Force Base in New York. I was a combat crew member in the Atlas F Missile program, assigned to a missile silo on a site in Dana Mora, New York. My duty as a missile combat crew member was to operate two generating power plants that supplied the electrical power to the missile silo and the Atlas F Missiles. After being stationed at Plattsburgh Air Force base for three years, I was given a new assignment, to Kunsan Korea Air Base in South Korea as a power production technician. I was assigned to the branch chief position in the Power Production Shop. The Kunsan Power Production Shop supplied emergency support electrical power generators to all essential base facilities during unscheduled power outages. I was also responsible for the runway block nine. This was a set of webbing that was attached to a B52 break drums stretched across the end of the runway to catch emergency aircraft or if an airplanes loss it landing gear or had break failure. During an emergency power outage, I used to set up and operated the emergency generators and water pumps. After finishing my tour in Korea, I was assigned to the 60th Strategic Bomb wing and the 49th interceptor squadron as a ground equipment repairman. I operated and repaired all associated equipment used to test and start aircraft. I was reassigned to Kwanju Korea during the Pueblo Crisis. The Pueblo Crisis was when the North Koreans captured one of our most highly classified communicating gathering ships. My job at Kwanju Air Base, Korea, was to run the generator set that supplied continuous power to the communication center. I was also involved in the building of Kwanju Air Base. I received the Expeditionary Medal for my tour in Kwanju. From Kwanju Korea, I was assigned to the 101st Fighter Interceptor Squadron station at Patrick Air Force base in Coco Beach, Florida. My job there was to receive and service incoming fighter aircraft for their return trip to their home base at Homestead Air Force in Southern Florida I left Sunny Florida on a reassignment to the 319th Fighter Interceptor Squadron in Grand Forks Air Force Base in North Dakota. I worked as a ground equipment repairman and became a member of the Chief of Maintenance Inspection Team. I ensured that all equipment assigned to an aircraft was in perfect working condition. In Grand Forks, I became an aide to Brigadier General Krause. From Grand Forks North Dakota, I was assigned to Bolling Air Force Base, in Washington D.C. to work as a general's aide for Lieutenant General Lebaily, the Inter-American Defense Commander until he retired. For the next 13 years I worked for the Nuclear Defense Agency Commander

Lieutenant General Warren D. Johnson, Lieutenant General Ronald Adams, and General Wilbert Creech the father and author of Total Quality Management. I am proud to have had the chance and opportunity to serve my country honorably in the United States Air Force.

BEES

I will never forget one summer day in Washington D.C. It was really hot and muggy, and a good day for picking blackberries. We would always welcome the hot weather after a cold hard winter. Nature took its course and all the trees and plants became alive with their beautiful shoots and blossoms. We would all anticipate the cherry blossom parade in the month of April. The cherry trees were a gift given to the American people from the people of Japan. The pretty white and pink blossoms on the trees in each yard were lined up in a straight row along the edges of the reflection pool surrounding the Lincoln and Jefferson Memorial. We also had cherry trees located in the front yards of homes located on Alabama Avenue between 15th Street and Congress Heights Street. When the blossoms came out on those trees, they covered the entire front yard. My sister and I used to walk up and down the block just admiring the beauty of God's creations. We would ask the owners if we could break off one or two limbs for our mother.

In the spring all the insects and bees would start foraging for food and building their nests and hives. I remember on two occasions we had yellow jackets that built their hives underground beside an old rotten log. They were very protective of their territory around their hive. If you came within five feet of the hive, an army of bees would attack you just for getting too close. We were mischievous little boys with nothing else to do but agitate the yellow jacket's hives. We used to run pass the hive with a stick and hit the log at the entrance to the hive. Approximately 100 to 200 bees would flare up in droves to attack anything that was moving close to the hive. One day we were messing with the hive, getting excited watching how the bees came out of their hive to attack whatever it was that disturbed the hive. On this particular morning there was an old lady who used to harass us when we played stick ball or football in the court, and our ball just so happened to end up in her yard. She would run outside get our ball and keep it. As she approached the corner where the beehive was, we ran past the hive and hit the log to disturb the bees. The bees went into action and attacked her as she past them at the corner by the log. She took off running and got stung by two or three bees. She never knew that we had disturbed the beehive. On one other occasion, Leon Robinson and I were out in the field picking blackberries. We saw this large yellow jacket hive in the center of the blackberry patch, located by all the large blackberries. We chucked a few bricks at the hive, and a mass of bees flew up to attack. Leon and I wanted to have some fun with the bees. We got our friend Lawrence, who always played jokes on us, and told him that we knew where some of the biggest blackberries in the world were. Lawrence got his little bucket and followed us back to the blackberry patch. The blackberry patch contained all sizes of berries. All the large berries grew in one spot, and everybody would look for the big berries because it would take less time to fill up your pot. We told Lawrence that we saw some big berries in the middle of the patch. He ran to the center to beat us there. Leon threw a red brick into the bushes as soon as Lawrence got in the middle, and the bees flared up and attacked Lawrence. He started to run out of the patch, and got half-way across the field, but the bees kept attacking him. We never laughed so hard, until we came across Lawrence lying down in the field covered with bee stings. We told him to get up because we thought he was playing like he was hurt. Lawrence didn't move. We turned him over, and saw that his whole body was blown up from the bee stings, and his face was like a basketball with no nose, eyes or lips. We ran across the street to get help. Lawrence's mother called the fire department rescue squad. We later heard that Lawrence had a 50:50 chance of surviving from the bee stings. Leon and I never told anybody what really happened. Lawrence survived, and to this day I am sorry for what we did to Lawrence. We didn't know how dangerous those yellow jackets were, and we never did it again. Lawrence, if you are still out there, I am truly sorry for what we did to you. It was unintentional. We thought we were playing a trick on you for fun, and didn't know the dangers that were involved. The lesson I learned is be careful and don't use God's creatures to play a joke on your fellow man.

HIGH SCHOOL CADETS

I believe some of the best parades in the country were held in Washington D.C. All of the district and local neighboring schools participated in most of the parades, and awards were given to the best marching bands, best float, best drill team and best school flag marchers. The cadets units from each school were given an award for the best marching military unit. When you entered High School in Washington D.C., you were enrolled in the military cadet program and issued an M-I rifle, and then assigned to a company and a squadron. You had to remember the serial number of your rifle and how to disassemble the rifle, clean it and put it back together in working order. We had to wear our uniforms on Tuesday and Thursday—drill days. We had to come to school at 6 am on those days for field inspection and cleaning our weapons. We had assigned to our regiment, one regular active duty Army Major, and cadet captains who inspected our cadet uniforms, shoes, hat and rifles. To get a passing grade, you had to march in one of the spring parades, participate in the city-wide military drill competition, and not miss more than three scheduled mandatory drill classes in uniform.

MY LOVE FOR TINA

One Sunday afternoon, Johnny Boy asked Eddie, Tyrone and me if we wanted to go with him to his Cousin Cleo's house on Sixtieth and East Capital Street in North East Washington D.C., next to the Maryland line. Johnny was going to see his girlfriend Betty Gene, and Tyrone and I went along for the ride. On our way back home, while sitting on the bus, this pretty little black girl came up to the bus window and said hello. I didn't know who she was, and the bus took off from the bus stop and headed for H & H Street N.E., where we could transfer to the street car and continue our journey home. All I could do was think about that pretty black girl with a full head of black hair. I saw her again when she came with Geraldine on a visit to Johnnie Boy's house. I was so shy I didn't say a word to her. I met her again when my family moved to the project housings on Fifty-Ninth and East Capital Street N.E. She lived on Fifty-Eight Street. Tina's sister G I and I used to hang out together with a group of teenagers who lived on Fifty-Eighth and East Capital Street. I had to pass her house on Sunday morning. Tina was always standing at the window in her kitchen, which faced the alley. When I came pass her house, I would always stop and hold a brief conversation with her. All of our conversations were about cooking. She would ask me how to cook something. This one particular Sunday, she had to cook some sweet potatoes, and I gave her a recipe. In turn, she said "You are going to make some woman a good husband." After that conversation, I used to try to talk to her every time I saw her. She used to hang out with an older group of people in their 20s. I remember the first time she let me kiss her, around the side of my house. My body went into a transformation. I heard her mother calling her. She told me she had to go, and she would see me later. The next time I remember seeing her was at the People's Drug Store, when she was on her way to school and I was on my way to work. We used to ride the same bus in the morning and transfer at H & H Street to catch the 92 Streetcar to North Capital Street. I would walk her to the Drug Store and buy her anything she wanted at the candy stand. I had a girlfriend named June, who used to attend Margaret Mary Washington School of Nursing with Tina. It was not long before June and I ended our relationship. Instead of going to work, I went downtown and joined the Air Force. One month later, I was on my way to Texas for basic training. After I finished training, I was assigned to Elmendorf AFB in Alaska. I came home on leave and wanted to go to a party. I called one of my friends, Johnnie May, to see if she wanted to go to the Coco Club, and it just so happened that Tina was over her house and answered her telephone. I asked if I could speak to Johnnie May, and she said "Is this you Charles?" I responded "Yes! Who may I be talking to?" She responded, "Tina! Don't you remember me?" I said "Yes!!" She asked me if I had any plans while home on leave. I told her I was going to the Coco club. She asked me if she could go with me, and would I take her out on a date. I was lying when I said yes to take her to the Coco Club, as I had no intention of taking her out on a date. We were partying in the Coco Club, when I looked over at the front door of the club and Tina was standing there. She was the prettiest woman in the club. I left for Alaska, and after two years I returned and was assigned to Plattsburgh Air Force Base in Plattsburgh, New York. I asked Tina if she would marry me and be my wife and she said yes. After our marriage, Tina came to Plattsburgh and had a nervous breakdown that lasted for about three years. I always re-member the vows I made in the rectory at the St Cyprian Catho-lic Church, "in sickness and in health, till death do we part". I have always stood by the vows I took when we got married. I did all I could during these trying first years of our marriage. I was determined it was going to work and was not going to al-low no devil from hell to break us up. All odds were against us from the start. We were told that we were unequally yoked. Our marriage was held in the rectory (a room in the priest's house) because I was a Catholic and Tina was a member of the Baptist Church. One thing good I received from the priest was a word of wisdom. If you tell the woman you married that you love her, every day, your marriage would last. I don't know how he knew that when priests don't marry. However, it is true, because as I write this book we have been married for 40 years, and I still love her with all my heart and soul. My love for her grows each and every day. God gave her to me on loan. I try very hard not to abuse her or bring shame on her by my actions. I try to give her anything she wants. Spoiling her is only the tip of the iceberg. I love her like a mother loves her baby at childbirth. I love my wife like God loves his creation. I love Tina like a garden loves rain. I love Tina like a preacher loves fried chicken. I love Tina like a cat loves a bowl of milk. I love Tina like a hog loves to wallow in mud. I love Tina like a fish loves a worm. I love Tina like a dog that loves a bone. I love Tina like God who so loved the world that he gave us his only begotten son. My dearest darling Tina, while sitting here thinking of nothing to do, I thought I would drop you a few lines or two. Never be angry with me darling, never be sorry that we have met. If you have loved another, I will help you to forget. I love you for who you are. We have overcome many obstacles during our years together. We have traveled on many occasions, threatening your own health. I love you for being the mother of my children. We had our ups and downs, but our ups far outweigh our downs. I have never regretted being married to you. You are my hope here on the earth, and Jesus is my hope after this life.

I would like to thank Mr. Brad Hill and Ms. Heather Ward for there help in reviewing my book.

I was awakened at 1: o'clock am on April 9, 2005 and inspired to write this transcript and express my thought on this unjust war we are in with Iraq.

War is Hell
April 9, 2005

It may not be what you want it to be
But it's a necessity for Freedom

War brings out the worst and best of us
War also bring s out the Best and worst of us

Do we or don't we like war?
Do we or don't we like Freedom?

I hate war that is necessary sometime
I love Freedom all of the time.

War has taken our best
Our best have secured our freedom

War is not a Godly act.
Love is.

War does not mix with love
Love does not mix with war
Love can prevent war.

Peace is puree love with no anger attached
Peace is love without war.

The absent of love is the missing ingredients that could
prevent a war.
Bring back love for our fellow man and there will have
peace throughout this land.

War is the result of Greed.
Peace is the absent of Greed
The war we are in should not be
Is our troops are dying each and every day to keep us free?

Billions of dollars are spent each and every day on oil
That is the main ingredients of this war

Is our troop's blood being exchanged for oil?

Look around you and you will see thousand of things are
made out of blood for oil in this great big sea.
Plastic bags, toys, car parts and clothes just to name a few
made from oil that we fail to see
Our purchasing of these items has an impact on the death
of our troop and the Iraq people overseas.

Would I allow one of my children to participate in this
unjust war?
Hell NO!! To the double time No!!! Not for just another
quart of oil.

We were taught to love and fight for freedom
Not to kill for the freedom to drive a car.

When I think and gather my thoughts on this unjust war
each and every day.

I hang my head and say why is it that our boys and girls, are
    dying in Iraq this way.
Why doesn't the American government confess?
It was George Bush and his daddy who got us in this
    mess.

I have been patriotic all of my life
Spending 24 years in the military service doing what I
    thought was right.
I have given total support to my country's views
I have the right to declare that this war in Iraq is unjust
    and ugly too.

I can not understand our way of fighting a war.
Our boys kill their enemy in self defense
And are prosecuted by our government for killing don't
    make since.

The political view on Iraq from our politician
What the hell is this?
Most of them have never served in a war zone such as this.

Those who challenge our troop's actions in the Iraq war,
Should themselves be prosecuted for treason that would
    even the score.

It is a shame that President Bush and his gang started this
    war.
Thousands of Mother's son and daughters are increasing
    the body count death score.

We never hear of the good news our troops have done.

Only the bad news that degrade our daughters and sons

Why are we seldom told when our troops are during their
    best?
Because this unjust war, it adds an increase in revenue for
    George Bush, Dick Chaney and the daily press.

Our Iraq brothers and our troops totally agree.

If it was not for George Bush, his father, Dick Chaney and
    the lies of mast destruction
This unjust war and killing in Iraq would not be.

Mother cry for the death of their daughters and sons.
Wives cry for the loss of a love one.

Children wonder and ask where their dad or moms have
    gone?

It is this unjust war being fought in Iraq that has taken
    them forever away from home.

Please! Please! let us end this tragic event.
To have peace again we must repent.

We have loss a generation of boys and girls to this war.
All because of our greed for oil.

I wish I could be President for one day.
I would stop the killing of Iraq people and bring our troop
    home today.

Is there any justification for the unjust war?
I do not think so it's all for oil.

Money!!! Money!!! Is all I hear that why we have been in
this unjust war for the pass couple of years.

Most of the American people want the unjust war to end.
But it those who will prosper for personal gains want this
bloody war of oil to continue without any shame.

Bush and Chaney can not see the coinage nor save this
country
Their mine is only on more oil and money

Bush and Chaney are just alike.
They don't have any of their family members in the Iraq
war to fight.

Bush and Chaney seem to have so much fun.
While American and Iraq mothers and fathers are burying
their daughters and sons.

If I could I would end this war.
To me it's like a pimp and his whore
Mr. Bush you as the pimp are able.
To release the Iraq people and our troop from your war
stables.
I do not foresee us winning this war
Just years and more years will increase our troop's dying
scores.

Our troops life is worth more then money

You President Bush and Dick Chaney can stop the coin-
    age.

Mr. President end this war and end it quick.
You can end this unjust war, you and Dick.

By Charles R. Hodge Jr.
April 9, 2005

Made in the USA
Middletown, DE
25 January 2017